ALSO BY GUY AND CANDIE CARAWAN

We Shall Overcome

Freedom Is a Constant Struggle

Ain't You Got a Right to the Tree of Life

Voices from the Mountains

VOICES FROM THE MOUNTAINS

Collected and recorded by
Guy and Candie Carawan

Alfred A. Knopf   New York   1975

THIS IS A BORZOI BOOK
PUBLISHED BY ALFRED A. KNOPF, INC.

Grateful acknowledgment is made to the following for permission to reprint
previously published material:

The Council of the Southern Mountains: for an excerpt from the Introduction
to *Mountain Path*, by Harriette Simpson Arnow.

The Dial Press: for an excerpt from *Divine Right's Trip: A Folk Tale*, by
Gurney Norman. Copyright © 1972 by Gurney Norman.

E. P. Dutton & Co., Inc.: for an excerpt from *My Land Is Dying*, by Harry M.
Caudill. Copyright © 1971 by Harry M. Caudill.

Grossman Publishers: for excerpts from *Death and the Mines*, by Brit Hume.
Copyright © 1971 by A. Britton Hume.

Harcourt Brace Jovanovich, Inc.: for an excerpt from Wendell Berry's essay
"Mayhem in the Industrial Paradise," from his book *A Continuous Harmony*.

Harper & Row, Publishers, Inc.: for excerpts from *Uptown: Poor Whites in
Chicago*, by Todd Gitlin and Nanci Hollander; and from *The Hurricane Creek
Massacre*, by Thomas N. Bethell.

Henry Regnery Company, Publishers: for excerpts from *Coaltown Revisited*,
by Bill Peterson.

Library of Congress Cataloging in Publication Data

Carawan, Guy.   Voices from the Mountains.

Bibliography: p.227   1. Appalachian region—Social conditions.
2. Appalachian region—Economic conditions.
I. Carawan, Candie, joint author.   II. Title.
HN79.A13C37   1975   309.1'74   74–7755
ISBN 0–394–48958–6
ISBN 0–394–70932–2 (pbk.)

This book is a collection of words, songs, and photographs from many
people, and it seems appropriate that the royalties benefit the growing
struggle for social change in the mountains. Therefore, the authors'
royalties will be contributed to an Appalachian community fund with an
emphasis on cultural projects. The fund is not intended for the personal
profit of individuals, but will be used for regionally oriented and
community oriented projects. It will be administered by the Highlander
Research and Education Center, New Market, Tennessee.

Manufactured in the United States of America

FIRST EDITION

CONTENTS

LIST OF SONGS

Appalachia has been viewed by many Americans as a place where change comes slowly and where people still live as they did one hundred years ago. As anyone who has lived here can verify, few things could be further from the truth. Within the past century major changes have come to the region, and today the Appalachian area is a highly industrialized segment of the larger American economy.

However, certain geographical and historical factors have combined to mold the rural population in the mountains into a people apart. The life of most Appalachian people is still heavily influenced by rural patterns of living. Almost 60 per cent of the population, or twice as many as in the rest of the country, still live outside metropolitan areas. The contrast in Appalachia between rural life and modern technological society is often vivid and dramatic: a home garden sometimes surrounds an oil or gas rig; modern highways may pass by log cabins; electric power lines cut huge swaths through valleys long isolated by rugged terrain. The industrial development of the region has always been uneven, concentrating in the broad river valleys and bottom lands and leaving the more rugged areas relatively untouched. Under these conditions it is natural that rural customs and values continue to have strong influence throughout the mountains. But the past few years have been marked by tremendous change, and the real story of Appalachia today is the attempt by mountain people to retain the humanistic elements of the old culture and at the same time to adapt to the pressures and demands of a technological society.

The Appalachian South is a vast area stretching from the tablelands of West Virginia and southeast Ohio to the rolling foothills of north Georgia. It contains three distinct sections: the plateau country, the Great Valley, and the highlands. The plateau country includes the central Appalachian coal fields, takes in part of the Allegheny Plateau in West Virginia and Ohio, and moves south to the Cumberland Plateau, which sweeps through eastern Kentucky, southeastern Virginia, and parts of east Tennessee.

The Great Valley splits the plateau country from the highlands. It begins with the level bottom lands and broad valley of the Shenandoah River in Virginia and extends down through east Tennessee. This section contains most of the manufacturing and small industrial plants along with the better farmland. The highland area includes the Blue Ridge Mountains and the Unakas, Balsams, and Blacks of Tennessee, North Carolina, Virginia, and Georgia. This is the most rugged section of Appalachia, with thirty peaks rising over 6,000 feet in elevation. Most of the jobs in this section come from textiles, lumber, and tourism.

Within the mountainous Appalachian South boundary of some 55,000 square miles, over 8.6 million people make their homes. Most have family ties to the land going back several generations. Almost 99 per cent were born in this country. About 6 per cent are black and live mostly in the industrial centers and towns. Less than 1 per cent are Native Americans.

For two hundred years the rugged mountain barriers of Appalachia served as a cultural barrier until the coming of electric power lines, new roads, and modern mass media opened up the region to more modern influences. The coming of mills, mines, and new industry after 1900 forced major changes in the old pioneer way of life. The past sixty years have seen the passing of most of the old ways. During the last twenty years the rate of change has accelerated. Consider these factors:

Very few people are alive today who know first-hand the pioneer ways of our ancestors. The leaders of most communities in Appalachia today are people who have been exposed to the influences of modern industry.

Farming, once the base of the old pioneer culture, has declined. Appalachia remains the stronghold of the small family farm, but most people now earn their income in wages or in payments from the federal government. Less than one fourth of the population earns a living from farming. Seventy-four per cent of all rural residents in Appalachia received some form of federal subsidy in 1970, compared to 54 percent for the rest of the nation.

Since 1944 over 2 million people have left the region—most of them from coal-mining areas, although lumbering and agricultural areas have also lost population. Since 1960 this out-migration has slowed down, but over 500,000 high-school graduates are expected to leave the area in the next ten years to find jobs. Unemployment in Appalachia averages 30 per cent higher than the rest of the country.

The coal industry has undergone drastic changes in markets and mining techniques. Today 150,000 miners produce approximately the same amount of coal as did 600,000 miners thirty years ago. Strip mining over the past twelve years has changed the entire nature of coal production. In 1960 strip mining accounted for less than one fourth of the coal produced in Appalachia; today it is the major method,

producing well over one half of all the coal mined in Appalachia and employing one tenth as many miners as are needed in deep mining.

The Tennessee Valley Authority, long regarded as the most responsive and progressive of federal agencies, has become a coal-consuming monster to produce cheap electric power. Strip-mine coal companies contracted by the TVA are destroying thousands of acres of mountain land—laying waste one section of Appalachia to light cheaply the homes and factories of another section. Only 10 per cent of the TVA's electric power is now produced by hydroelectric facilities.

The Army Corps of Engineers has assumed control of most watersheds within the region. In 1972 a report issued by the corps, in co-operation with other federal agencies, called for the construction of two hundred new dams primarily to provide water and recreation benefits for metropolitan centers outside Appalachia. Dams are already a major disrupter of Appalachian life and have forced thousands of families to be uprooted from their family homesteads. Forty-four dams are planned for eastern Kentucky alone, although recent federal studies have shown that existing lakes and rivers in the coal fields are rapidly dying because of acid mine drainage and sedimentation from strip mining.

The Appalachian Regional Commission (ARC), a federal agency with broad administrative powers regarding federal spending in Appalachia, has begun reorganization of local county governmental units in a plan that may bring about the greatest change in local government since the Revolutionary War. The ARC concept establishes multicounty planning units with governing boards composed of elected officials, businessmen, and civic leaders. The boards have veto power over all federal funds, creating a new level of bureaucracy removed and insulated from the democratic process of direct election by the people.

The development of second homes and huge tourist centers by land speculators has sent land rates and taxes skyrocketing since 1960, making it harder for natives to hold on to their homes. This trend has hit elderly people particularly hard since they often live on fixed incomes; their children have migrated to find work, and the old people must either submit to a lower standard of living because of inflation or sell their homestead and obtain a "nest egg" rather than become a financial burden to their children. While the scarcity of fuel caused by the energy crisis may slow down this exploitative use of land, the demand for recreation and "escape" areas from the cities seems to ensure a continuing increase of land rates.

The U.S. Forest Service has continued to acquire more mountain land under its management and ownership. In 1930 the Forest Service had seven national forests within the region and a total of 2,462,015 acres of land. By 1964 there were nine national forests lying primarily within the southern Appalachians and over 11,365,000 acres owned by the U.S. government. The Forest Service, in 1970, owned over 14 million acres in Appalachia. Since the government has the right of eminent domain in acquiring land for national forests, there is little choice for the individual mountaineer but to move and begin life elsewhere.

The growing power of the federal government combined with the ruthless practices of the coal, textile, and timber industries has, in recent years, raised the specter of a huge industrial park or "hillbilly" reservation extending throughout Appalachia, peopled only by a few maintenance workers and ruled by federal or corporate managers who refuse to let native mountaineers remain on the land. Stripped of the coal and timber, it is dotted with lakes in which only tourists can swim. In the midst of all these trends the individual mountaineer has little opportunity to counter the pressures of the federal government or large corporations. The pattern of outside interests controlling the region is a familiar one to anyone who has studied mountain history. Appalachia has always been a domestic battleground with conflicting forces trying to gain control of the rich natural resources. Native Americans were driven off their ancestral land by waves of white pioneers who swept across the hills in a never-ending flow. Behind the pioneers came land speculators representing rich eastern investors who desired vast expanses of new land. Later still came the railroads and the corporations that opened up the region to industrial exploitation around the turn of this century. Along with the industrial barons were missionaries of the major American churches seeking new converts and new domains. With the advent of the War on Poverty and the expansion of federal programs within Appalachia, a new type of missionary has descended upon the region.

It is not surprising, then, that many rural mountaineers have adopted a wait-and-see attitude toward new developments, looking with well-warranted suspicion upon anyone who promises a new and better way of life. To mountaineers survival has meant acquiring patience and a sense of perspective about the pressures of modern life. Like most Americans, we have changed when it seemed in our best interests to do so. In this respect, we are no different from our ancestors.

The early white settlers of Appalachia came here from Europe to escape the powers of church and state. Along the eastern seaboard, where large landowners and the state Church of England were already firmly entrenched, they found similar abuses; so they moved west where land was cheap. Most were Scotch-Irish and English, with a scattering of Dutch and German.

In 1774 (two years before the Declaration of Independence) mountaineers said in the Watauga Declaration they were free from the English king; they fought against slavery in the 1800s, believing that no man had the right to own another; they became a national symbol of a militant union movement during the 1930s; and they have always sent a disproportionate share of young men off to war. But today the region is in the hands of absentee corporations. The recent coming of cheap electric power, new roads, and public schools has not meant that local government is more responsive to the needs of people. Instead, improvements have been made only when they would be profitable to the industries of the region. Rural Appalachia has always suffered from a one-industry economy, whether it be coal, textiles, or lumber; and the political power has usually been concentrated in the hands of old, established families who form the core of the local business community or of the new managerial groups that run the industrial plants. Local wealth is also concentrated in the hands of a few—only 9 per cent of the population earned more than $10,000 in 1970.

What does the future hold for the people of Appalachia? It is evident that real progress cannot be made until large numbers of people begin to share in the decisions that affect all of us. So far the most effective attempts to build new political forces have come from the central coal fields, where union members have used their years of experience working within their own organizations. The mountaineers who migrated north and then returned home brought back with them valuable experiences in organization and leadership. For democratic change to come to the region, all of these skills and experiences are needed. Unfortunately most of our college-educated people have either left the region or have returned to take jobs which perpetuate the economic and political exploitation that an increasing number of moun-

taineers oppose. The small middle class in the mountains is usually tied closely with local industry and has given little support to recent efforts to bring about change.

Over the past ten years the most effective leaders in Appalachia have emerged from working, disabled, or unemployed people, and a new coalition of power is at work among many of these grass-roots organizations. Union organizing techniques have long been known in the more industrialized sections of the mountains, particularly in the coal fields, but these techniques and the tremendous collective energy behind them have traditionally been applied only to the industrial workplace. In recent years, though, these techniques have been applied to organizing communities for common goals. The first significant attempts to do this since World War II came from the struggles of black people in the South who were fighting for equal rights. Their leaders combined union-organizing ideas with the tremendous motivation of a people who were determined to obtain political freedom and equality. The struggles centered around the concept of "community" rather than the centralized workplace of the mine and mill or the core of a political party.

Most of the people in this book have been influenced deeply by either union organizing or community organizing. They have one thing in common—they saw a problem in their own community or workplace and tried to solve it through direct group action. Through their combined efforts they are changing the very nature of Appalachian society. The roving pickets of the early sixties, the anti-strip-mine movement that followed the pickets, the development of grass-roots community organizations in the War on Poverty, the rise of welfare-rights groups, and the reform battles of the UMWA have all left their mark upon the collective face of Appalachia.

In the past few decades new elements have been introduced into the traditional framework of Appalachian life— elements that must be considered when we talk about what the future of the region might be. Most writers on the region have chosen to emphasize the hopelessness of the area rather than the many examples of people striving to improve their lives. To truly understand the events of the past few years it is necessary to look at the men and women who have worked in the tunnels of the mines, the lint-filled spinning rooms of the mills, and the steep, forested hills. The price of personal integrity has been great and they have paid for it with suffering and sacrifice, with sleepless nights and pain written long upon wrinkled brow. Few of these people are well educated; many are old, physically sick, disabled, and untrained for modern jobs. Some of these individuals are found within this book. Others await attempts to seek them out and to learn from them the real history of the mountains. To find them we must look outside the educational programs of schools and the mass media, for these institutions are controlled by the same corporations and forces that now control our natural resources and our people. The stories of the individuals within this book should help in that search.

For those of us who are from Appalachia, who love it, and who want to remain, these people offer valuable insights and feelings about what it means to be a mountaineer in a modern technological society. And for the reader who may not live in Appalachia, there is much to be learned here from present attempts within the mountains to build a more democratic society. Welcome to the developing Free State of Appalachia.

MIKE CLARK

Highlander Center
New Market, Tennessee

A NOTE ABOUT THE SONGS

The collection of songs in this book is varied. Not all are indigenous to the mountains. A few were written by visitors and recent arrivals. Some are by people with roots in the mountains who now live elsewhere. Some are by well-known singers and song writers and some are by community people who were moved by a specific situation to voice their feelings in a song. Some are by new young song writers.

Old ballads and religious songs have been given new words and meanings. Newer bluegrass and country-style songs tell of the murder of Joseph Yablonski and the destruction of Paradise in Muhlenberg County. "Amazing Grace" and "Bright Morning Stars," long sung in mountain churches, have become anthems at many community gatherings around social issues.

In 1967, when we came to live and work in eastern Kentucky, we heard few songs and little singing that dealt with the social and economic problems affecting people's lives, but in seven years the situation has changed dramatically. Along with the increase of grass-roots activity, there has been a growing body of songs that deal with these struggles and feelings.

This book is a sampling of the songs that are drawing people together in struggle, in pain, and in celebration.

GUY and CANDIE CARAWAN

Highlander Center
New Market, Tennessee

Voices from the Mountains

I CAN FEEL THE SWEET
WINDS BLOWING

I CAN FEEL THE SWEET WINDS BLOWING

WORDS AND MUSIC: BILL STAINES

© 1974 *Sweet Wine Music*

I can feel the sweet winds blowing thru' the valleys & the hills
I can feel the sweet winds blowing as I go, as I go
I can feel the sweet winds blowing thru' the valleys & the hills
I'm a-going home to Jesus, bless my soul, bless my soul.*

I can see the morning breaking thru' the valleys & the hills, etc.

I can feel a touch of heaven thru' the valleys & the hills, etc.

I can hear the people singing thru' the valleys & the hills, etc.

I can feel the people stirring thru' the valleys & the hills, etc.

* Alternative last lines:
   (1) I'm a-going home to freedom, bless my soul, bless my soul.
   (2) I'm going home to Carolina, bless my soul, bless my soul.
   (3) I'm going home to West Virginia, bless my soul, bless my soul.

MOUNTAIN STREAM

WORDS AND MUSIC: JOAN BOYD

When it's just cold e-nough___ to make me ting-le when I breathe And the air holds me close like a lov-er at___ my sleeve And I'm feel-ing free and cool as if I'm part of what I see And I know I could-n't speak and ev-er say the way I feel when I See a moun-___tain stream, run-ning full and run-ning free Say-ing ___ come ___ and___ sing with me. Do you feel___ it pound ing in___ your heart? Do you feel___ it run ning through your veins? Do you ___ feel___ it cool-ing off___ your mind? Do you feel___ it rush–ing, Rush ing a-way___ with your soul, ___ Rush–ing with___ ___ your ve – ry soul? ___

D.C.

When it's just cold enough to make me tingle when I breathe
And the air holds me close like a lover at my sleeve
And I'm feeling free and cool as if I'm part of what I see
And I know I couldn't speak and ever say the way I feel
    when I
       See a mountain stream, running full and running free
       Saying come . . . and sing with me.
       Do you feel it pounding in your heart?
       Do you feel it running through your veins?
       Do you feel it cooling off your mind?
       Do you feel it rushing,
       Rushing away with your soul,
       Rushing with your very soul?

Running, running over rocks, and through the roots of golden birch
See it trickle over here, see it lurch over there
I feel the spray in my face and crystal dampness in my hair
As I stand all alone and let my heart teach me a song
    that is
       Here as in a mountain stream, running full and running free, etc.

Hear it straining, humming low, from its mountain emerald head
As it glimmers over ice in a sparkling winter bed
Or in rhododendron spring, hear it make the mountain ring
As it roars and rushes down with laurel blossoms in its crown
    It's a
       Sparkling mountain stream, running full and running free, etc.

*Farmer in eastern
Kentucky*

I was born on June the thirteenth, 1899, in eastern Kentucky. I was raised on a farm with domestic and wild animals. Sheep, hogs, and cattle roamed wild in the forest. We raised what we ate and slept in dilapidated houses. We enjoyed nature in all of its aspects and knew no doctors or surgeons. Mountain dew was our principal medicine.

I knew the whistle of the ground hog, the call of the crow, the songs of the birds, the cunning of the fox, and the squall of the bobcat. I knew the art and expertise of teaching an oxen to put his neck to the yoke and to kneel down low when his load was too heavy. These are things that can't be taught in the classroom.

The mountains of eastern Kentucky were a vast domain, rich in the abundance of nature to sustain domestic and wild animals. The timberlands, valleys, mountains, and streams were a Garden of Eden where the lamb lay down with the lion. There were no barbed-wire fences to restrain men. The mountain man knew how, as the Indian did, to live off the land. At this time there were no phonographs, no radios, no television, no automobiles, no railroads, no public highways, no airplanes. Our highways were buffalo trails made by wild animals and later on used by the Indians and white adventurers. Freight boats traveled the Kentucky River to transport the necessaries of life to Hazard and Whitesburg.

I lived through the aftermath of the mountain feuds when father was committed against son and brother against brother. I lived by the code of the mountains. I lived in an age when people respected honor and truth, where a liar was scorned and ridiculed and a man who would not pay his debts was considered an outcast.

When the railroad pushed up the valley from Jackson to Hazard and on to McRoberts, it marked the beginning of the end of a way of life for a group of rugged men and women who had the nerve and the courage to traverse the mountain barriers and establish rugged individualism—known as the mountain man.

—EVERETTE THARP

Kris Mendenhall

9

WON'T YOU COME AND SING FOR ME

WORDS AND MUSIC: HAZEL DICKENS

I feel the sha-dows now up-on me
And bright an-gels beck-on to me Be-
fore I go, dear Christ-ian broth-ers,
Won't you come and sing for me

CHORUS
Sing the hymns we sang to-geth-er In that
plain lit-tle church with the bench-es all worn
How dear to my heart, how pre-cious the
mo-ments We stood sha-kin' hands and sing-ing the
songs. My

I feel the shadows now upon me
And bright angels beckon to me
Before I go, dear Christian brothers,
Won't you come and sing for me
    Sing the hymns we sang together
    In that plain little church with the benches all worn
    How dear to my heart, how precious the moments
    We stood shakin' hands and singing the songs.

My burden is heavy, my way has grown weary
And I have traveled a road that was long
But it would cheer this old heart, good sisters,
If you'd come and sing one song.
    Sing the hymns we sang together, etc.

In my home beyond that dark river
Your dear faces no more I will see
Until we meet where there's no more sad partings
Won't you come and sing with me.
    Sing the hymns we sang together, etc.

It was always very nice at the end of church when every-body would just kind of mill around and shake hands with each other. Everyone was very humble and warm with each other. There was always a lot of hugging going on, and that scene impressed me very much.

—HAZEL DICKENS

Kris Mendenhall

When I went out to teach in 1926 there were hundreds of roadless creek valleys all through the Southern Appalachians, and almost no roads at all in Eastern Kentucky. . . .

. . . The best homes were usually the older log houses, and around these log houses there were many pleasant things including much that was beautiful; for those who like open fires, hounds, children, human talk and song instead of TV and radio, the wisdom of the old who had seen all of life from birth to death, none of it hidden behind institutional walls, there was a richness of human life and dignity seldom found in the United States today. . . .

. . . The hills are still there—that is most of them— though strip mining and super highways have taken their toll. Yet the life of the twenties and thirties that revolved about the communities in the shut away valleys is gone. One can walk for miles and miles through the upper reaches of the creek valleys and find only tumble-down houses, often the chimney alone, a rusted post office sign wind-lodged in a young pine tree, or a leaf-choked spring, around it scattered blocks of stone to remind the passerby that once a spring-house stood there. . . .

. . . The world I first saw in the summer of 1926 is gone; it cannot be excavated and re-created. And anyway, who can excavate a fiddle tune, the coolness of a cave now choked with the water of Lake Cumberland, or the creakings and sighing of an old log house?

—HARRIETTE SIMPSON ARNOW

Earl Palmer

I was born and grew to adulthood in Big Lick, Tennessee, near the headwaters of Daddy's Creek and the Sequatchie River. That is the spot of earth I still call home and if choices were ours, that is where I would choose to die.

. . . Appalachia is my land and hillbillies are my people. My roots go deep in the mountains. Some of my ancestors were among the first white settlers in the mountains. Except for a few brief years at school and work, I have spent my entire life in the hills of Tennessee, Pennsylvania, and Kentucky. I think of myself as an Appalachian.

There is much in traditional mountain culture worth cultivating and emulating. Mountain people have valued simple adequacy rather than super abundance, over consumption, and waste. They have a capacity to honor friendship and neighborliness above influence and power. They have a tendency to adapt rather than to manipulate.

I used to think that what was needed was to bring mountain people into the "economic mainstream." I thought it would be possible to do this and still preserve some of the positive, humanizing qualities of mountain cultures. I no longer think that this is either possible or desirable. Our challenge is not to join mainstream America. It is to re-create a renewed and authentic form of what the mountains have always been. From the time that the first white settlers deliberately cut their ties with the coastal culture of colonial America to start a new life in this wilderness, the mountains have offered an alternative to mainstream America. This alternative is nearer to being absorbed today than it has ever been in the past. The task before us is to renew this alternative and endow it with the capabilities (including an adequate economic base) it will need to survive in late-twentieth-century America.

I was home again Christmas. Once again I thrilled to the rush of the white water of Daddy's Creek at Sutton's Ford. I breathed the smogless air of the high plateau and warmed my soul on the frosty sight of snow high on Hinch and Bear Den Mountains. I remembered how my daddy used to say he liked the mountains because he needed something to rest his eyes against.

—MIKE SMATHERS

THE COMING OF THE ROADS

WORDS AND MUSIC: BILLY EDD WHEELER

Oh now that our mountain is growing
With people hungry for wealth
How come it's you that's a-going
And I'm left alone by myself?

We used to hunt the cool caverns
Deep in our forest of green
Then came the roads and the taverns
And you found a new love, it seems.

    Once I had you and the wild wood
    Now it's just dusty roads
    And I can't help from blaming
    Your going
    On the coming
    The coming of the roads.

Look how they've cut all to pieces
Our ancient poplar and oak
And the hillsides are stained with the greases
That burn up the heavens with smoke.

We used to curse the bold crewmen
Who stripped our earth of its ore
Now you've changed and you've gone over to them
And you've learned to love what you hated before.

    Once I thanked God for my treasure
    Now, like rust, it corrodes
    And I can't help from blaming
    Your going
    On the coming
    The coming of the roads.

The coming of the roads has brought very basic changes to mountain life over the years. Some of the recent developments—strip mining, land speculators developing the region for tourists, the Appalachian Regional Commission's "land use plans" designed to move people out of the hollows and into towns—are making it increasingly difficult to remain a mountaineer.

. . . These people, especially the old timers, have endured a lot to earn the right to live as they see fit. How would it feel to be away for a while and come home to be told that Mom, Dad, Aunt, Uncle, Grandma and Grandpa, sister or brother had been relocated 40 miles or so distant for their "own good, of course"? And when you get there, you find them all crowded in a little community, dissatisfied and having to pay for what once was paid for, such as water, sewage facilities, and heat—even for a roof over their heads. Or, you could be charged an admission to walk up your favorite hollow where you were raised, only now it's a recreation area, a tourist attraction, another way to get that almighty dollar at someone else's expense. The old saying "The almighty dollar is the root of all evil" is not a myth any more, but a true fact.

—RELON HAMPTON

Overleaf: *Kentucky farmer Cecil Combs*

I. THEY CAN'T PUT IT BACK
The Struggle Against Strip Mining

I was born and raised in eastern Kentucky and I love the land of eastern Kentucky. I've run over the hills and looked at the beautiful sights. But it's no beautiful sight to see our hillsides destroyed—tore up—and our water streams polluted. People run from whole logs rolled up against their houses. Sayin' take it and like it.

I'll fight agin' it as long as there are breath in this man's body.

—GEORGE TUCKER

The hills of Appalachia are bleeding. Strip mining for coal has gouged deep and gaping gashes. The guts of our once proud mountains have been ripped out and dumped into the gullies. When you fly over the Appalachian area, you see entire mountaintops which have been scalped off. Other hills have been laterally peeled all the way around like an apple. Thousands of miles of ugly high walls stand starkly against the horizon.

—REP. KEN HECHLER,
West Virginia

This is the cheapest kind of mining, but it does the most damage. Reduced to essentials, it consists of blasting and bulldozing the top off a mountain to expose the coal seam that lies beneath, and then loading the coal into trucks and carting it away. The relocated mountain top winds up, by force of gravity, in the valleys below. After a heavy rain, it becomes mud and moves like lava until it reaches the bottom of the valley, where it slides into streams, becomes silt, and is washed through the tributaries of eastern Kentucky into the Kentucky River, and then the Ohio, and the Mississippi, and finally into the Gulf of Mexico—where a great deal of eastern Kentucky lies today.

—THOMAS N. BETHELL

20

BLACK WATERS

WORDS AND MUSIC: JEAN RITCHIE

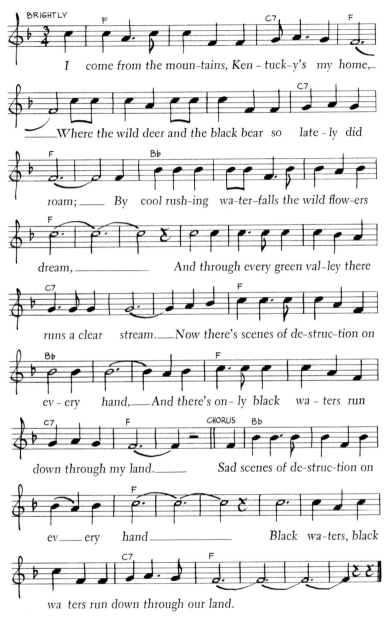

I come from the moun-tains, Ken - tuck-y's my home,—

____Where the wild deer and the black bear so late - ly did

roam;____ By cool rush-ing wa-ter-falls the wild flow-ers

dream,_____ And through every green val-ley there

runs a clear stream.__Now there's scenes of de-struc-tion on

ev - ery hand,__And there's on - ly black wa - ters run

down through my land.____ Sad scenes of de-struc-tion on

ev ____ ery hand _____ Black wa-ters, black

wa ters run down through our land.

© 1967, 1971 by Geordie Music Publishing, Inc. Used by permission.

I come from the mountains, Kentucky's my home,
Where the wild deer and the black bear so lately did roam;
By cool rushing water-falls the wild flowers dream,
And through every green valley there runs a clear stream.
Now there's scenes of destruction on every hand,
And there's only black waters run down through my land.
    Sad scenes of destruction on every hand
    Black waters, black waters run down through our land.

O the quail, she's a pretty bird, she sings a sweet tongue;
In the roots of tall timbers she nests with her young.
But the hillside explodes with the dynamite's roar,
And the songs of the small birds shall sound there no more.
And the hillsides come a-sliding so awful and grand,
And the flooding black waters rise over my land.
    Sad scenes of destruction on every hand;
    Black waters, black waters run down through the land.

In the rising of the springtime we planted our corn,
In the ending of the springtime we buried a son,
In summer come a nice man, said, "Everything's fine—
My employer just requires a way to his mine"—
Then they threw down my mountain and covered my corn,
And the grave on the hillside's a mile deeper down,
And the man stands and talks with his hat in his hand
As the poisonous water spreads over my land.
    Sad scenes of destruction on every hand;
    Black waters, black waters run down through the land.

Well, I ain't got no money and not much of a home;
I own my own land, but my land's not my own.
But if I had ten million—somewheres thereabouts—
I would buy Perry County and I'd run 'em all out!
Set down on the bank with my bait in my can,
And just watch the clear waters run down through my land!
    Well, wouldn't that be like the old Promised Land?
    Black waters, black waters no more in my land!

23

Robert Cooper © 1972

I have seen it in print and I have heard it directly from strip operators that the mountains must be ruined for the benefit of what they call "the rest of the nation." A Letcher County operator told me personally that West Virginia and eastern Kentucky had to be sacrificed, written off. I am certain that from Washington to Frankfort to Charleston to Richmond and Columbus they will not find the Appalachian sacrifice too great a tragedy; the tragedy is ours; the profits belong to them.

When we speak of the coal industry we do not at all mean all the people in it. We mean big coal, big corporations, absentee owners, holding companies—all those big enough to collectively buy courts and legislators—and maybe governors. We want a healthy deep-mining industry in which men work as safely as the underground may be worked —mining in which human beings are more important than corporation profits.

—WARREN WRIGHT

These people, I call 'em establishment bullies—the robber barons, the coal barons—came into the colony of Appalachia. Appalachia is a colony in the truest sense of the word. It has all the earmarks—the absentee landlords; nothing built of permanence. You can look at the whole area—the poor roads, the poor schools, the lack of facilities—and realize that there's no solutions, and no planning for any solutions, for the poor colony of Appalachia.

I think what has happened in other areas can show you what will happen to us when profit from the coal is gone. These entire valleys will be flooded for tourism and cheap power. They've been so impatient with us for their profits all along, it's just like they've been engaged in a war with us. It looks like we've been in an atomic war, and losing badly. They've destroyed our hillsides; they've destroyed our streams.

I've said time and again that there is a class of men on the face of the earth who works in the filth and grime and dreadful noise and danger of a coal mine; that they deserve to be able to come out to their homes and drop down in the stream and fish, if that's what they want to do, or go into the woods and hunt, if that's their pleasure, they should be allowed to. But that's all been destroyed.

—JOHN TILLER

Disabled miner Ellis Bailey of Clear Fork, West Virginia, has been active in the anti-strip-mining movement.

26

Earl Dotter

This is the day of the giant bulldozer, the hideous grinding auger, machinery of the strip miner, and the smoke and dust of them hang over the ridges and hollers of eastern Kentucky like a pall of sorrow. This is the time when all the sins of past generations have caught up with us.

For my Grandpa Hall, it was an unwitting sin. He, along with most of his neighbors, sold the mineral rights to his land to the friendly, likable man who said he represented a company that thought there might be a little coal on our land worth getting out. The company was willing to take a big chance and pay Grandpa 50 cents an acre and, since Grandpa had more than a thousand acres, this amounted to around $500, a handsome sum in those days. For a man with a dozen children, it was also impossible to refuse.*

—JEAN RITCHIE

* The land companies would in turn lease portions of a coal seam to the coal operators, receiving a royalty on each ton of coal mined. Today their holdings in the area are worth an estimated $7,200 an acre in coal royalties alone.—DAVID WELSH

27

SAD THE DAY

WORDS AND MUSIC: JIM GARLAND

Sad the day——when I saw the steam shov-els a-com-in' The clank of their wheels as they clattered along Deep in my heart—— a voice seemed to be say-ing Good-bye my sweet home, you soon will be gone.(In eighteen and) gone. Leave 'em a lone, please—— do not dis—— turb them Don't dump the vel-low clay mud o-ver their graves Al-though the law may say you have a right to Be-cause of that twen-ty-five cents that you paid. This house it

Sad the day when I saw the steam shovels a-comin'
The clank of their wheels as they clattered along
Deep in my heart a voice seemed to be saying
Good-bye my sweet home, you soon will be gone.

In eighteen and eighty my folks were rejoicing
They'd sold the mineral rights on the farm
For twenty-five cents an acre they sold them
My folks didn't know they would do any harm.

Leave them alone, please do not disturb them
Don't dump the yellow clay mud over their graves
Although the law may say you have a right to
Because of that twenty-five cents that you paid.

This house it was the home of my father
His father and mother, they lived there too
Now they all lay asleep beneath the green willow
Along with their wives and children so dear.

I looked on the hill and I saw the steam shovel
Dumping that clay dirt over the hill
Soon every living thing will be covered
My beautiful valley soon will be filled.

Leave them alone, please do not disturb them
Don't dump the yellow clay mud over their graves
Although the law may say you have a right to
Because of that twenty-five cents that you paid.

Don't force me to leave this house I was born in
Don't force me to leave the land dear to me
Just take back the twenty-five cents that you gave them
And just go away, and please let us be.

About eighty years ago the big land companies of the East sent their agents into this part of eastern Kentucky to buy up all the mineral rights from the people who live here. They ended up eventually with about 90 per cent of the acreage in most of the east Kentucky counties, having paid a price of 25 cents to 30 cents for each acre. They did this by a legal instrument known as the *broad-form deed* that gave the mineral owner all the minerals under the ground; gave him the right to extract these minerals without any liabilities whatsoever for damages to the surface of the land.

The most that was in the people's minds at that time probably was that someday in the future, some mining company would come in and sink a shaft or introduce a deep mine. Now we've seen, years later, the introduction of violent and destructive strip-mining methods that uproot the trees and the people and just generally destroy the mountains and the acreage that's here now.

Kentucky is the only state where the courts have ruled in favor of the mineral owner on the broad-form–deed question.

It's really hard to believe that eighty-some years ago the husband and wife who signed that deed with an "X" could really envision what the results of their actions would be.

—J. T. BEGLEY,
attorney

Mike Clark

29

It is not possible to talk about strip mining in the mountains without considering the impact which TVA policies have had upon the entire coal market.

Around 1960 TVA opened negotiations with East Kentucky strip miners to see if they could supply cheap coal in large quantities to the TVA. Richard Kelly and Bill Sturgill, owners of the Kentucky Oak Mining Company, the largest strip mining company in East Kentucky, were chosen. Kelly and Sturgill, in close co-operation with TVA, began to experiment with various methods of mining coal using large scale surface mining equipment for the first time in East Kentucky. The largest coal auger ever built, with a diameter of seven feet, was constructed and a five year contract for two and one half million tons of coal per year was signed in 1961 with Kelly and Sturgill. This contract, for the first time, made large scale strip mining economically feasible in East Kentucky because it gave a stable economic base for five years. . . . Using the methods and equipment pioneered by Kelly and Sturgill (and engineered by TVA people) strip mining began to spread across the face of Appalachia's coal fields.

TVA must share a major portion of blame for the destruction of Central Appalachia. However, in our eagerness to attack what appears to be the soft underbelly of TVA because of its public ownership, we must remember that the major private utilities use the same methods of obtaining electric power. They would like nothing better than to see TVA set up as a public scape goat for the entire industry.

—MIKE CLARK

To see stripping on a really vast scale, you have only to move to Paradise, in western Kentucky. Here, thousands of acres of land are being stripped by the Peabody Coal Company. What Peabody strips, the Tennessee Valley Authority burns to produce electricity. Peabody is both the country's largest coal company and largest producer of strip-mined coal. TVA —an agency of the federal government—is the country's largest consumer of strip-mined coal.

TVA destroyed the entire town of Paradise to build the world's largest steam-generating plant, the Paradise Steam Plant. The only thing TVA did not destroy at Paradise was the Smith Cemetery. The living were ejected; the dead still wait their fate. TVA has buried the living in eastern Kentucky; they are now exporting the process to other areas. Every buried and destroyed landowner in Appalachia owes TVA his wrath. If TVA did not destroy him directly, they helped to make it all possible.

If TVA had decided in the sixties to buy deep-mined coal, we would now have a safe deep-mine industry—not one run ragged by strip-mine competition.

—JAMES BRANSCOME

PARADISE

WORDS AND MUSIC: JOHN PRINE

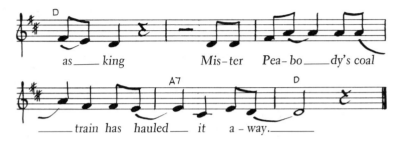

When I was a child, my family would travel
Down to Western Kentucky, where my parents were born
And there's a backwards old town, that's often remembered
So many times, that my memories are worn.
>And Daddy won't you take me back to Muhlenberg County
>Down by the Green River where Paradise lay
>Well I'm sorry my son, but you're too late in asking
>Mr. Peabody's coal train has hauled it away.

Well sometimes we'd travel right down the Green River
To the abandoned old prison down by Adrie Hill
Where the air smelled like snakes, and we'd shoot with our pistols
But empty pop bottles was all we would kill.
>And Daddy won't you take me back to Muhlenberg County, etc.

Then the coal company came with the world's largest shovel
And they tortured the timber and stripped all the land
Well, they dug for their coal till the land was forsaken
Then they wrote it all down as the progress of man.
>And Daddy won't you take me back to Muhlenberg County, etc.

When I die, let my ashes float down the Green River
Let my soul roll on up to the Rochester Dam
I'll be halfway to heaven with Paradise waiting
Just five miles away from wherever I am.
>And Daddy won't you take me back to Muhlenberg County, etc.

Down in Muhlenberg County and parts close by, John Prine's song "Paradise" is something of a hit. One store manager in the area says he sold 600 to 800 copies of a recording of the song in three weeks or so. Local radio stations have given the song heavy play. According to one disc jockey, "The response on the whole has been tremendous. We had a lot of coal miners call up early in the morning, before they go on shift, and request it."

Prine was born and grew up in the Chicago area, but he used to spend summers at an uncle's home in Paradise, where his grandfather and father grew up, and he witnessed the stages of the town's decline and fall.

—Louisville *Courier-Journal & Times*, January, 1973

In the name of Paradise, Kentucky, and in its desecration by the strip miners, there is no shallow irony. It was named Paradise because, like all of Kentucky in the early days, it was recognized as a garden, fertile and abounding and lovely; some pioneer saw that it was good. ("Heaven," said one of the frontier preachers, "is a Kentucky of a place.") But the strip miners have harrowed Paradise, as they would harrow heaven itself were they to find coal there. Where the little town once stood in the shade of its trees by the river bank, there is now a blackened desert. We have despised our greatest gift, the inheritance of a fruitful land. And for such despite—for the destruction of Paradise—there will be hell to pay.

—WENDELL BERRY

33

Jeanne M. Rasmussen

Hanna Coal Company, with a huge strip-mining operation in Southeastern Ohio, attracted national attention in 1973 when it blocked Interstate 70 for three days so that its monster shovel "the Gem of Egypt" could be moved across the highway to continue mining south of the interstate. "Gem" stands for Giant Earth Mover; "Egypt" for the Egypt Valley which Hanna has destroyed in the past few years.

—MIKE CLARK

The machine weighs approximately 14 million pounds; has a bucket with a capacity of 130 cubic yards. It cost approximately $7 million to erect the machine. The machine operates twenty-four hours a day, seven days a week, 364 days a year. It is idle on Christmas.

The Gem is really a coal mine in itself. It produces, or uncovers, approximately 2¼ or 2½ million tons of coal a year.

—RALPH HATCH,
President, Hanna Coal Co.

STRIP AWAY

WORDS: MIKE KLINE AND TOM BETHELL
MUSIC: "SWING LOW, SWEET CHARIOT"

Strip a way,____ big D-9____ Do____zer, co-min' for to bu-ry my home,____ I'm a get-tin'____ mad____der as you're get-tin' clos____er, Com-in' for to bu-ry my home. Well I looked up – a spoil bank – and what did I____ see?____ Com-in' for to bu-ry my home,____ The Is-land Creek Coal-Com-pa-ny push-in' down-my trees,____ Com-in' for to bu-ry my home.

© 1969 by Michael Kline (words)

Strip away, big D-9 Dozer, comin' for to bury my home,
I'm gettin' madder as you're gettin' closer,
Comin' for to bury my home.

Well I looked up a spoil bank and what did I see?
Comin' for to bury my home,
The Island Creek Coal Company pushin' down my trees,
Comin' for to bury my home.

They're goin' to turn our mountain homeland to acid-clay,
Comin' for to bury my home,
To make a cheaper rate for the TVA,
Comin' for to bury my home.

Strip away, big D-9 Dozer, comin' for to bury my home,
I'm gettin' madder as you're gettin' closer,
Comin' for to bury my home.

Well, boys, we gotta organize against them stripmine men,
Comin' for to bury our homes,
And the broad-form deed that always lets them win,
Comin' for to bury our homes.

Strip away, big D-9 Dozer, comin' for to bury our homes,
We're all gettin' madder as you're gettin' closer,
Comin' for to bury my home.

Strip mining, while it is going on, looks like the devil, but . . . if you look at what these mountains were doing before this stripping, they were just growing trees that were not even being harvested.

—AUBREY J. WAGNER,
Chairman of the Board of TVA

Doug Yarrow

Reclamation* is a farce. In eastern Kentucky they're bull-dozing down the tops of the mountains to create flatlands. In western Kentucky they're digging out the bowels of the earth to create mountains.

In eastern Kentucky the strip miners, under Kentucky law, are required to spend only $500 to reclaim an acre of strip-mined property. In Great Britain and West Germany, two of the countries to which we export strip-mined coal from eastern Kentucky, they do not even allow contour strip mining, such as we have in the mountains. But in their flatlands, which are potentially more reclaimable, they require

that an amount of from $4,000 to $6,000 per acre be spent.

So we're bulldozing down our mountains in eastern Kentucky to sell cheap coal to the British and the West Germans, who refuse to allow their land to be treated this way.

—JAMES BRANSCOME

* All of the Appalachian states have laws requiring reclamation. Reclamation is an attempt to restore strip-mined land to its original condition or to a condition in which the land can have some useful purpose. This process minimally involves grading the area and planting acid-tolerant vegetation.

You know damn well those pine trees the governor planted didn't live over a week. It's like trying to put makeup on a cadaver and making believe it's alive.

—DONALD MACINTOSH

NATURE'S LAMENTATION

WORDS AND MUSIC: BILL CHRISTOPHER

You all have heard of the nine pound hammer
And how it makes the moun-tains roll?
Strip-per, strip-per, spare that tree A-
las, he did not heed Per-haps a tree shall
grow a-gain But a moun-tain has no seed.

You all have heard of the nine pound hammer
And sixteen tons of hard-rock coal
But have you heard of the stripper's shovel
And how it makes the mountains roll?

Bulldoze away the trees and topsoil
Drill and blast away the stone
Dip out the coal and load that tandem
Leave the spoil, the stripper's gone.

    Stripper, stripper, spare that tree
    Alas, he did not heed
    Perhaps a tree shall grow again
    But a mountain has no seed.

A million years to make a mountain
A hundred years to grow a tree
A few short days with a big bulldozer
Will send it all down to the sea.

    Spare that mountain, spare that tree
    Alas, he did not heed
    Perhaps a tree shall grow again
    But a mountain has no seed.

They say that man must have black diamonds
To make the steam that makes the juice
But stripper, harken unto wisdom
To get an egg don't kill the goose.

    Stripper, stripper, spare that tree
    Alas, he did not heed
    Perhaps a tree shall grow again
    But a mountain has no seed.

    Spare that mountain, spare that tree
    Alas, he did not heed
    Perhaps a tree shall grow again
    But a mountain has no seed.

A meeting of the Citizens' League to Protect Surface Rights, Blackey, Kentucky

It would take an upheaval—a new re-creation of this earth—to put this country back like it was before the modern methods of strip miners came on it.

There's a law in this land that says you and I can have children. There's another law that says you can't destroy your children. There's a law that says a man can buy and own land. But there ought to be a law that says that man couldn't destroy the land . . . because he owns it only temporary.

My grandmother was a full-blooded Cherokee Indian. I think I owe my grandmother something. I don't think her folks would have appreciated destroying the environment. The environment was their living. They had no other way to make it.

There's no other way for people to stay here in Appalachia unless we protect the environment. And that's something we're certainly going to do and I think we ought to work together. This is a job for all of us. And I think it can be done. We need to start at the top—the big boys first. They can afford to lose. A poor man can't afford to lose. He's got nothing to lose except his life. And I think he's willing to put it on the line. I don't think he's got any choice . . . now. We're gonna have to put it on the line.

—JOE BEGLEY

Phil Primack

Strip mining began on a large scale around 1961 in East Kentucky. By 1964 large areas of Pike, Knott, Harlan and Letcher Counties had been gutted. In Knott County small landowners formed the now legendary Appalachian Group to Save the Land and People. They took miners to court, held off bulldozers with their bodies and finally with their guns. The coal companies ruled the land but not the people.

In small meetings at churches, community centers, in homes and occasionally at court houses, the Appalachian Group continued its fight. Membership increased—usually spurred on by the sounds of diesel engines on a nearby ridge. As months passed it became clear that the only farms saved from strip mining were places where small landowners, family and friends, were willing to physically stop the stripping machines. Almost without exception the courts backed the coal companies, not the small landowners.

—MIKE CLARK

Bill Strode

In 1965 "Widow" Combs, a frail sixty-one-year-old Knott County woman with a twenty-acre farm, lay down in front of a bulldozer to protect her mountain farm and was promptly carried off the hill by law officials to spend Thanksgiving in jail.

—MIKE CLARK

Bill Strode

In 1965 "Uncle" Dan Gibson, an 81-year-old Baptist preacher and coffin-maker in Knott County, rallied people when he took a gun and stood off strip miners to defend the land of his grandsons who were in the military services. Gibson was arrested by a party of state policemen but only after his neighbors agreed to defend his property while he was in jail. Gibson was taken to Hindman, the county seat, and promptly released when the town filled up with armed mountain men and women who were determined to see that no harm came to Uncle Dan.

—MIKE CLARK

THE BALLAD
OF DAN GIBSON

WORDS: GURNEY NORMAN

The foreman of the 'dozer crew
Told old Dan he was comin' through
To scrape away his trees and earth
And strip-mine coal for all he was worth.

Dan looked at the 'dozer and then at the fellow,
Said Buddy you're wrong if you think I'm yellow.
Don't think that because I'm an old man
I'm afraid to defend my piece of land.

The driver of the 'dozer had a second thought.
He began to wonder just whether he ought
To tangle with as fierce a looking man
As the one before him they called old Dan.

So he said to Dan, now listen mister,
I drive this 'dozer for my wife and sister.
I ain't drawing a big enough pay
To die for no boss and the TVA.

So let me tell you what I'm going to do,
I'll go and get the boss of this strip-mine crew.
Then if you two are bound to fuss
Why that'll be better than the two of us.

The foreman went to Hazard and got the boss,
Told him he was scared their cause was lost.
If we don't do something about old Dan
We'll never get to strip-mine any more land.

The stripper could hardly believe his ears.
For how could a man of eighty years
Defy an industry as powerful as coal?
The stripper couldn't see it to save his soul.

But still old Dan had him sort of worried
So out to the mine-site the boss-man hurried,
Afraid that he might lose some face
If he didn't put Dan back in his place.

It won't be easy, the foreman said.
Dan's got a strange notion inside his head,
That just because his land is his,
He can keep out the strip-mine biz.

Now you couldn't say the stripper was a cowardly fellow.
It wouldn't be fair to call him yellow.
It was just to keep peace in the mountain tops
That he took along with him twenty-one cops.

When the boss arrived with his well-armed band
He strutted out on old Dan's land.
Hey Dan! he yelled. Are you up there?
Come on down, we'll settle this fair.

For the next few minutes everything was still
While the cops and the boss-man stared at the hill.
They were looking for the man they called old Dan
To arrest him for trespassing his own land.

They waited a while, and then fanned out
To assault the hill and try to rout
This dangerous criminal who had defied
Some powerful men now after Dan's hide.

The hill was steep and to the big boss
The surface of it was a total loss.
But he knew that under the rugged soil
Lay a seam of coal worth more than oil.

So he urged the cops with their clubs and guns
To find old Dan and make him run
Till he was off the strip-mine site,
And don't worry too much about his legal rights.

Old Dan wasn't hard for them to find.
The cops could have found him if they'd been blind.
For Dan wasn't the kind to cringe and hide,
He figured the law was on his side.

But the boss said Dan, that's where you're wrong.
The law's on the side of him that's strong.
That's why us coal men are all so lucky
To mine in the Commonwealth of Kentucky.

Dan could hardly believe his ears.
His bright old eyes filled up with tears.
He wasn't afraid to go to jail,
But he couldn't stand to think that freedom had failed.

The strip-miner said Now don't cry, Dan.
Let's make us a deal for this here land.
If you let me strip this worthless hill,
Me and my partners will pay you well.

Dan looked around him at all the cops.
Then he gazed a while at the mountain tops.
He saw the ugly strip-mine bench,
Then frowned at the boss like he smelled a stench.

Said, you got this coal through a crooked deed
To satisfy your lust and greed.
You cheated my family of the mineral rights
But you'll never get the surface without a hard fight.

So they took old Dan to the Hindman jail,
But he got out on a sudden bail
Put up by his neighbors and all of his kin
So he could fight the strip-miners again.

Dan's fighting them now, with a thousand others
Who in this war are all blood-brothers,
Bound to defend each other's land
From the ruin of the evil strip-mine band.

Mike Clark

I came to the creek 20 years ago. The hills were covered with game. You could kill five squirrels in an hour. Now you can't hear a quail call anywhere.

. . . The timber's gone, the wildlife's gone and the water's gone. I've tried to save what I could, but I hate to think this is what this country is "leaving my grand children."

The strip miners are killing these old hills. When they finish, there won't be anything left. My ancestors lived here, and I've got a stepson in Vietnam who wants to come back here and live out his days too. Yes, sir, this is my land—and my land is dying.

—DAN GIBSON

Bill Strode, Louisville Courier-Journal & Times

On June 29, 1967, Jink Ray and some neighbors, members of the Appalachian Group to Save the Land and People, blocked with their bodies bulldozers that were about to start stripping Ray's land on Island Creek, a Pike County community. They managed to stop temporarily the Puritan Coal Company. Then, in the noisy publicity that followed, Governor Edward Breathitt intervened.

Jink told the governor he had built his house with his own hands, and built everything on his farm. If they stripped up above his land, the first rain would wash everything he'd done with his life down the creek. They might as well wash him with it. He wasn't going to see it all go. The governor promised to help.

The next day was a major confrontation. Jink was faced with a court order not to interfere, and the strippers were to come across his land that day. All his neighbors came out in spite of the court order and the bulldozer was stopped. Jink sent a telegram to the governor telling him, "If you intend to help us, please do it now." The governor finally did take away the strip operator's permit. And they have never come back. It was an isolated victory for strip mining's opponents in Kentucky.

—JOE MULLOY

THE BALLAD OF JINK RAY

MUSIC: "PRETTY BOY FLOYD"
WORDS: JIM W. MILLER

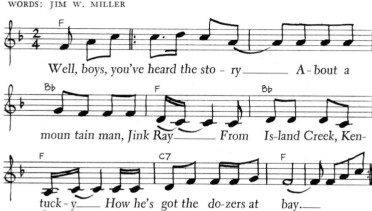

Well, boys, you've heard the sto - ry___ A - bout a
moun tain man, Jink Ray___ From Is-land Creek, Ken-
tuck - y___ How he's got the do-zers at bay.___

© 1971 by Jim Miller

Well, boys, you've heard the story
About a mountain man, Jink Ray
From Island Creek, Kentucky
How he's got the dozers at bay.

It was early one June morning
When Jink first made his stand
Against the company dozers
To save his house and land.

They came from the Puritan Coal mines
To strip his land away.
Jink was waiting with his neighbors
They were with him all the way.

Jink turned the lead bulldozer
Standing firm and resolute
But the man from the Puritan Coal Mines
Said, "Tomorrow we'll go through!"

They were waiting there next morning
To defend Jink's property line.
When the law won't do it for you
You got to do whatever you can.

Jink was waiting on the mountain
With his neighbors in a force
When the deputy sheriff served papers
To bring Jink into court.

Yes, the company's got an injunction
To get Jink out of their path,
To cross his land with dozers
And ruin his trees and land.

Does the broad-form deed they're holding
Give the Puritan Company right
To destroy Jink's stand of poplars?
The judge has to decide.

Does the broad-form deed they're holding
In any way justify
Killing fields with acid run-off
Washed down in a tide?

Does it justify their sending
Tons of stinking rock and mud
Washed down in the valley
In a reeking, poison flood?

Does it justify their forcing
Jink to leave the land he owns,
That he's farmed and tended faithful
Since 1921?

You may say, "Let Jink fight it,
It's no skin off my nose!"
But when any man's rights are dozed down
Why, boys, all of us lose.

What if they make this one cut
On the mountain of our rights?
In time the slope comes sliding
And sours our way of life.

Men residing in northern cities
Enjoying our wealth
Have been leaving us for years now
To hunker in their filth.

You may ask, "Well, what can we do?"
And I say, Support the Group
To Save the Land and People
And we'll come out on top.

You've read it in the papers,
You've seen it on TV.
Now boys, let's stand together
And kill the broad-form deed!

In an opinion handed down on June 21, 1968, by the Kentucky Court of Appeals, the hopes of the Appalachian Group and its supporters were crushed. In substance, the majority held that the owner of underlying minerals may totally ruin the surface of the earth without the consent of the man who owns and tills it—and without paying him anything for his loss!

Few Kentucky lawyers were surprised by the decision, but among thousands of mountain families it deepened the hopelessness of the old and the cynicism of the young.

—HARRY M. CAUDILL

The ineffectiveness of law, combined with the negative rulings in the Courts, seems to have left strip mining's foes no gentlemanly way to fight the industry. In Kentucky, that means trouble. The technique that Jink Ray used to save his land requires great patience, tremendous publicity and a sympathetic governor. Most Kentuckians don't have the temperament for that kind of fight. Basically, they are inclined to think that long court battles are too risky and the science of publicity too obscure. Black powder is louder and simpler to handle, and the end results are more satisfying.

—THOMAS N. BETHELL

A bill designed to negate the broad-form deed was finally passed by the Kentucky legislature in March of 1974. It requires the surface owner's written consent before issuance of state strip-mining permits. However, the bill does not take effect until January 1, 1975, to allow time for a court test, since the broad-form deed's legality has always been upheld by Kentucky courts.

Anti-stripping sabotage. A steam shovel and pick-up truck were among the casualties in a 1968 dynamiting of strip-mining equipment in Bell County, Kentucky. In this incident, one of many involving sabotage, damage was estimated at $750,000.

SOWIN' ON THE MOUNTAIN

ADAPTATION OF TRADITIONAL MOUNTAIN HYMN:
GUY CARAWAN AND GEORGE TUCKER

Sow-in' on the moun-tain, reap-in' in the val__ley,__
Sow-in' on the moun-tain, reap-in' in the val__ley,__
Sow-in' on the moun-tain, reap-in' in the val__ley,__
You're gon-na reap just what you sow.

Sowin' on the mountain, reapin' in the valley,
Sowin' on the mountain, reapin' in the valley,
Sowin' on the mountain, reapin' in the valley,
You're gonna reap just what you sow.

Look at what their greed has done to our mountains,
Look at what their greed has done to our mountains,
Look at what their greed has done to our mountains,
You're gonna reap just what you sow.

Tell that liar he better quit his lying,
Tell that liar he better quit his lying,
Tell that liar he better quit his lying,
You're gonna reap just what you sow.

Tell that strip miner he better quit his stripping,
Tell that strip miner he better quit his stripping,
Tell that strip miner he better quit his stripping,
You're gonna reap just what you sow.

Stripping on the mountain, polluting of the valley,
Stripping on the mountain, polluting of the valley,
Stripping on the mountain, polluting of the valley,
You're gonna reap just what you sow.

Brothers and Sisters, don't you get weary,
Brothers and Sisters, don't you get weary,
Brothers and Sisters, don't you get weary,
You're gonna reap just what you sow.

Help your friends, they're gonna need you,
Help your friends, they're gonna need you,
Help your friends, they're gonna need you,
And someday you'll need them too.

Sowin' on the mountain, reapin' in the valley,
Sowin' on the mountain, reapin' in the valley,
Sowin' on the mountain, reapin' in the valley,
You're gonna reap just what you sow.

Robert Cooper © 1972

I'll tell you something that happened in our area. They were starting stripping on Bull Creek. The people there had had a few meetings. And at this one meeting they had a whole houseful of people and they had some lawyers there. They were trying to decide what they could do to stop the stripping on Bull Creek.

So one of the lawyers said, "Well, there ain't much you can do. They got a broad-form deed which makes it legal. I don't see anything you can do." And these people just dropped their heads; they were so discouraged.

I said, "People, are you all going to sit on Bull Creek and let them strip your land away and cover your house up?" I said, "You needn't come all the way out here and talk to a lawyer—they'll all tell you the same thing." I said, "Where's your shotgun and where are you all at? Get together and get after those strippers and you can stop them from stripping your land. While you're around here trying to get you a lawyer, you can have 'em run out of Bull Creek." I said, "I think anybody's low life that lets 'em bury them alive. I'd kick and scratch as long as I could." I told them, "If you wait for legislation, you won't have nothing left on Bull Creek. It'll be too late then. You better get back home and do it now."

And they every one rallied. They jumped up and slapped their hands and said, "That's what we want to hear. That's what we want to hear. Can we do that?"

I said, "It's been done. We've done it . . . why don't you try it and see?" I said, "If you need me, call me. And I'll bring everybody that wants to come."

And a lot of people stuck up their hands and said, "You can count on me."

And they went back and they run them strippers off of Bull Creek. They didn't strip and they've never come back. And they had a big strip operation planned for Bull Creek. Later on the people told me, "We didn't need to call you; we run 'em off." And they said, "We've stopped it on Bull Creek; we'll go to the next creek. Just let us know when they start and we'll be there."

I'll tell you, the strip operators is not the bravest people in the world. They've not got that much support in the community. The only thing they've got is each other. A lot of people that really works on a strip job won't back his operator if a showdown comes. We've got a law that says you can shoot in self-defense. It *is* self-defense when a stripper comes to bury you. If he'll jump a fence, don't shoot him—as long as he's gone.

—EULA HALL

Women temporarily stop strip mining in Knott County, Kentucky, by blocking machinery, February, 1972.

THEY CAN'T PUT IT BACK

WORDS AND MUSIC BY BILLY EDD WHEELER
THIRD VERSE ADDED BY MICHAEL KLINE

back._____ can't put it back,

Down in the valley 'bout a mile from me
Where the crows no longer fly,
There's a great big earth-movin' monster-machine
Stands ten stories high.
The ground he can eat, it's a sight;
He can rip out a hundred tons at a bite.
He can eat up the grass, it's a fact,
But he can't put it back!

They come and tell me I've got to move,
Make way for that big machine;
But I ain't a-movin' unless they kill me,
Like they killed the fish in my stream.
But look at that big machine go;
Took that shady grove a long time to grow.
He can rip it out with one whack,
But he can't put it back.

I never was one to walk in lines,
Picket with placards, or carry signs.
But maybe I'm behind the times.

You can bet your sweet life you're goin' to hear from me;
I ain't a-goin' to take it layin' down,
'Cause I'm tired of seein' rocks that bleed
On the bare guts of the ground.
And I ain't a-sellin' my soul
So they can strip out another tiny little vein of coal.
And I ain't a-movin' out of my tracks,
'Cause they can't put it back,
They can't put it back.

The strip-mining industry has been guilty of raising the dead and they're burying the living. And this we can't let happen any longer. We're still living. Let's don't let them bury us any longer.

—BESSIE SMITH GAYHEART

54

Bessie Smith Gayheart and Madge Ashley

Phil Primack

II. AIN'T GOIN' HOME SOON
Leaving the Mountains to Look for Jobs

We nearly starved to death down there last winter. Things aren't much better here, but I wouldn't go back. I sure do miss the hills, though.

—ANNA BLAND,
from Clarksburg, West Virginia,
now a resident of Chicago's Uptown

Nobody wants to leave the mountains—which is remarkable considering how hard it is to live in the mountains. But they all wind up going, whether they want to or not.

—JOHN ARMS

COAL TATTOO

WORDS AND MUSIC: BILLY EDD WHEELER

Trav-el-in' down that coal town-road; Lis-ten to my rub-ber tires whine. Good-bye to buck-eye and white syc-a-more I'm leav-in' you be-hind. I've been a coal man all my life Lay-in' down track in the hole.__ Got a back like an iron-wood bent by the wind; Blood veins blue as the coal.

Phil Primack

Travelin' down that coal town road;
Listen to my rubber tires whine.
Good-bye to buckeye and white sycamore
I'm leavin' you behind.
I've been a coal man all my life
Layin' down track in the hole.
Got a back like an ironwood bent by the wind;
Blood veins blue as the coal.

Somebody said that's a strange tattoo
You have on the side of your head.
I said that's the blueprint left by the coal.
Just a little more and I'd been dead.
But I love the rumble and I love the dark.
I love the cool of the slate.
But it's travelin' down that new road lookin' for a job,
This travelin' and lookin' I hate.

I've stood for the union, walked in the line,
Fought against the company.
I've stood for the U.M.W. of A.,
Now who's gonna stand for me?
For I got no house and I got no pay,
Just got a worried soul
And this blue tattoo on the side of my head
Left by the number nine coal.

Some day when I'm dead and gone
To heaven, the land of my dreams,
I don't have to worry about losin' my job
To bad times and big machines.
I won't have to pay my money away
And lose my hospital plans,
I'm gonna cut coal while the blue heavens roll,
And sing with the angel band.

59

AIN'T GOIN' HOME SOON

WORDS AND MUSIC: BILLY EDD WHEELER

It's been a long___ time since I___ been home. It's been a long___ time since I___ been home.___ It's been a long___time since I___ been home.___ And I ain't___ goin' soon, no I ain't go-in' back soon. I was born in a coal camp, stars at my head, And moun-tains as far as I could see. Got to work ev-ery day and I made a big pay___There was hon-ey in the horn for me. And the coal dust blowed, like a dark sum-mer snow But I don't hear the roar of the tip-ple an-y more Or the whine of the trucks on the line. Now the town's all

It's been a long time since I been home.
It's been a long time since I been home.
It's been a long time since I been home.
And I ain't goin' soon, no I ain't goin' back soon.

I was born in a coal camp, stars at my head,
And mountains as far as I could see.
Got to work every day and I made a big pay
There was honey in the horn for me.
And the coal dust blowed, like a dark summer snow
But I don't hear the roar of the tipple any more
Or the whine of the trucks on the line.

Now the town's all gone, it's gone away.
The town's all gone, it's gone away.
Now the town's all gone, it's gone away.
The people are straw the wind has blowed away.

I was born in a holler that was lonesome and long
Where the sun didn't shine all day.
But the banjoes in the night and the stars' big light
Was pleasures that I wanted to stay.
How could anybody know that the next year or so
We would all be a-travelin' over the mountain and plain,
Tryin' to plant our roots again?

It's been a long time since I been home.
It's been a long time since I been home.
It's been a long time since I been home.
And I ain't goin' soon, no I ain't goin' back soon.

Hell, some counties around home, I'll bet they double their
population on weekends. I know twenty or thirty guys from
right around my home who come back most every week
and bring their families with them.

—TOM DUFF

Louisville Courier-Journal & Times

. . . Instead of being migrants, many of them are just long-distance commuters. Instead of actually going north and taking their families with them and putting their roots down up there, these guys will go up and get a job in a factory and then come back every week end. What they're actually doing is commuting 600 miles to work.

—JOHN ARMS

A RECOLLECTION

That car of Daddy's was an old Pontiac he bought with the first wages he ever earned in Cincinnati. It had over a hundred thousand miles on it when he got it, but he never hesitated to take off in it for Kentucky. The first year we lived up there we never missed a week end going home. Fifty-two round trips in a year, over two hundred miles each way, six, seven, sometimes eight and nine people in it every run. Every Friday as soon as Daddy'd get home from work we'd load up and head out, and drive six straight hours south on old U.S. 25, through Lexington and Richmond, east into the hills on 421, then down state route 666 to the homeplace in Finley County.

In the wintertime it would be dark before we even set out, but in the summers the light would hold 'til almost Richmond, and I remember the programs that came on the radio about that time of day. My daddy played the guitar some, and he loved hillbilly music, and so at six o'clock he'd tune in the Hillbilly Hit Parade out of WCKY in Cincinnati. I remember it started and ended with somebody's fierce picking of the "Steel Guitar Rag," and then when it was over Wayne Rainey and Lonnie Glossen would come on, trying to sell harmonica instruction courses. Wayne and Lonnie were good musicians too, and when they'd get wound up Daddy would get excited and start to sing along with them, and bounce around in his seat and beat on the steering wheel with his hand. He'd cut up like that for miles and miles. He'd tickle us all so much we'd forget how uncomfortable we were, piled on top of one another in the back seat of that old car.

On Fridays you wouldn't mind being uncomfortable because you knew you were on your way to someplace you really wanted to be a lot, but on Sundays you'd feel so blue about having to leave the homeplace to go back to Cincinnati there wasn't any way in the world to get comfortable and Daddy would have to stop every hour or so and let people out to stretch. We hated it, coming back, but then it was only five more days 'til we'd go down home again, and we cheered ourselves up with that thought.

—GURNEY NORMAN

63

THE GREEN ROLLING HILLS OF WEST VIRGINIA

WORDS AND MUSIC: BRUCE PHILLIPS
VERSES 3 AND 4: SALLY WORCESTER
VERSE 5: HAZEL DICKENS AND ALICE GERRARD

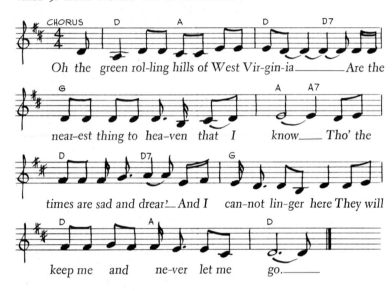

© 1973 *by Bruce Phillips*

Oh the green rolling hills of West Virginia
Are the nearest thing to heaven that I know
Tho' the times are sad and drear'
And I cannot linger here
They will keep me and never let me go.

My daddy said don't ever be a miner
For a miner's grave is all you'll ever own.
Well it's hard times everywhere,
I can't find a dime to spare,
These are the worst times I've ever known.
    Oh the green rolling hills of West Virginia, etc.

So I'll move away into some crowded city
In some northern factory town you'll find me there.
Tho' I leave the past behind
I will never change my mind.
These troubled times are more than I can bear.
    Oh the green rolling hills of West Virginia, etc.

Well I traveled to a crowded northern city
So far away and lonesome for my home
There were no jobs anywhere
And I could not linger there
So I started out once more to search and roam.
    Oh the green rolling hills of West Virginia, etc.

While traveling all around the open country
Finding people in the same sad shape as me,
This one lonely thought came clear,
We've got nothing left to fear,
We must fight and win the battle to be free.
    Oh the green rolling hills of West Virginia, etc.

But someday I'll go back to West Virginia
To the green rolling hills I love so well
Yes, someday I'll go home and
I know I'll right the wrongs
And these troubled times will follow me no more.
    Oh the green rolling hills of West Virginia, etc.

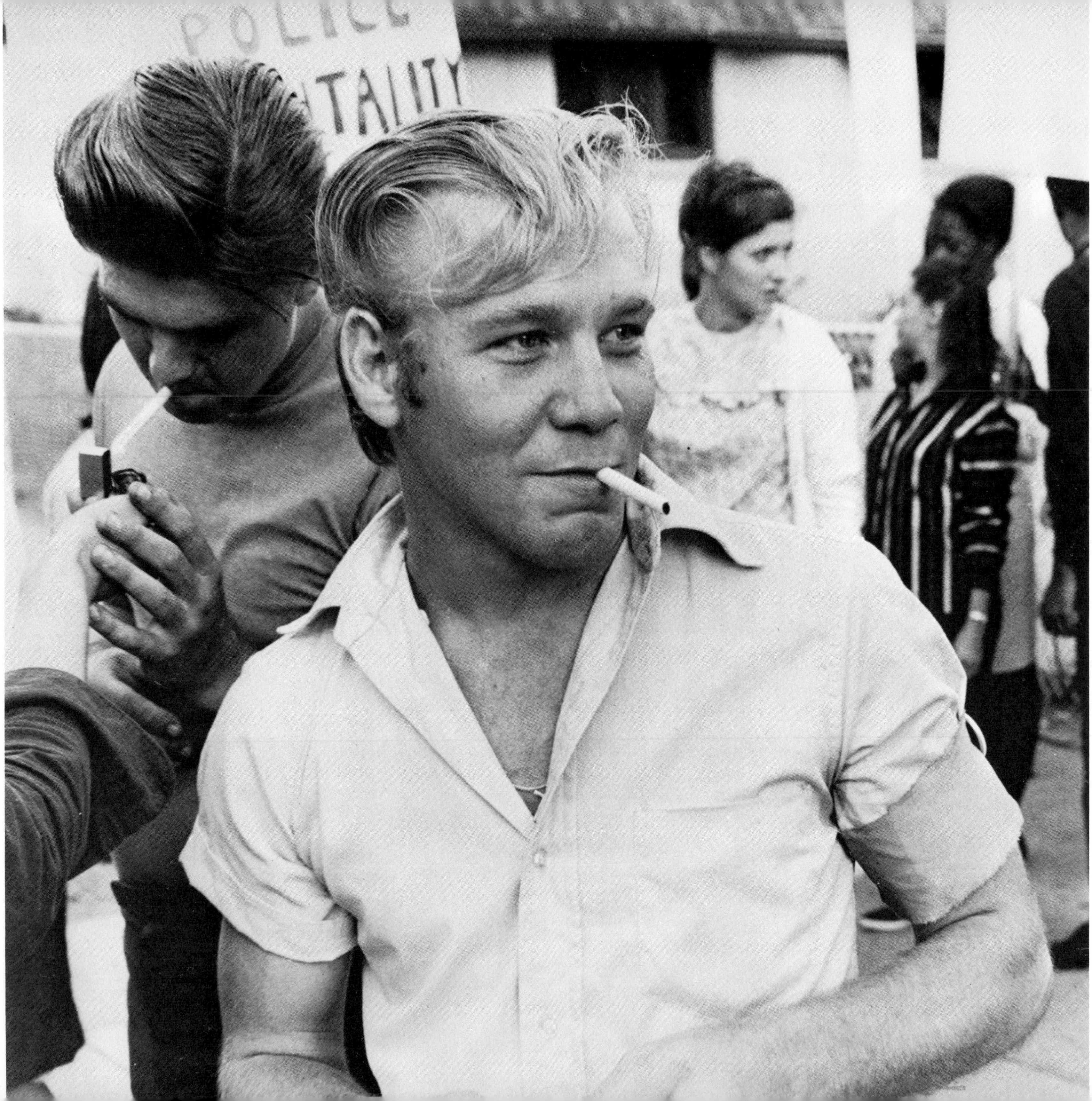

Nanci Hollander

Peter O'Callahan

I went to New York when I was fourteen to work in a government canning factory. The factory sent somebody down to recruit people to go up there and work. And they'd take anybody who said they was eighteen. They didn't care. They took three or four busloads. And when we got up there we worked and worked and worked and they never paid us. We was supposed to be getting 40 cents an hour, but we never did get a payday. When we went we understood they were paying for our bus ticket. But their excuse for not paying us was that they were withholding our transportation and our board and things.

They were getting free labor and making pigs out of us. They gave us the jobs that nobody else would do.

We were about to starve out and we were going to organize that plant—bunch of hillbillies, didn't know the procedures of organizing or calling a strike. None of us had ever been out of the county, hardly. We knew nothing of picket lines or unions or striking. We just knew we were getting rubbed wrong and we was going to do something about it. We learnt fast.

They called it inciting to riot. Lord have mercy! In five minutes they had enough police and state troopers and paddy wagons till they was throwing us in there on top of each other. I never was stomped and treated no worse in my life.

They got us to the police station and some of us got six months on the rock pile—those that was eighteen. Luckily I was fourteen. They looked at me and they said, "How old are you?"

I said, "I'm eighteen."

He said, "You couldn't be. Where's your birth certificate?"

I said, "I don't have one."

He said, "We gotta get in touch with your parents."

That scared me when he said that.

He said, "You oughta be in the schoolhouse."

I said, "I graduated from the eighth grade last year."

They kept us overnight and the next day put us on the Greyhound bus for Pikeville—the ones that was underage.

—EULA HALL

JENNY'S GONE AWAY

WORDS: RICH KIRBY AND MICHAEL KLINE
MUSIC: TRADITIONAL

Jen-ny's gone a-way,___ Jen-ny's gone to
O-hi-o___ Jen-ny's gone a-way.
Jen-ny's wear-ing strings and rags Jen-ny's gone a-
way___ Jen-ny's wear-ing strings and rags
Jen-ny's___ gone a-way.

Jenny's gone away, Jenny's gone to Ohio *
Jenny's gone away.

Jenny's wearing strings and rags
Jenny's gone away
Jenny's wearing strings and rags
Jenny's gone away.
    Jenny's gone away, etc.

Jenny was a pretty gal, don't you know
Jenny's gone away
Worked until her hair turned grey
Jenny's gone away.
    Jenny's gone away, etc.

Jenny's hill got stripped away
Jenny's gone away
Strip mine operators had their way
Jenny's gone away.
    Jenny's gone away, etc.

Starvation was her baby's fate
Jenny's gone away
The caseworker said she was a burden to the state
Jenny's gone away.
    Jenny's gone away, etc.

The army took Jenny's brother today
Jenny's gone away
He'll come home in a pine box and stay
But Jenny's gone away.
    Jenny's gone away, etc.

Jenny's man died in the Farmington mine
Jenny's gone away
Company insurance didn't treat her so kind
And Jenny's gone away.
    Jenny's gone away, etc.

Jenny didn't want to go away
Jenny's gone away
The company took her place to stay
And Jenny's gone away.
    Jenny's gone away, etc.

* In alternative choruses substitute "Cleveland town," "Detroit town," "Baltimore," etc., for "Ohio."

I felt terribly inferior when I came to the city. People were always putting down my accent. I was very confused about my identity and what my role was, anywhere. I was quite lonely actually. I just didn't know how to fit in. . . .

If I mentioned anybody that I liked or respected in the music field, nobody knew who I was talking about, unless I was talking to somebody who came from back home. . . . Everything I heard on the radio was popular music or something like that, and I thought, well, that went along with my new life. . . . That's what I was supposed to sing; so I started trying to sing that popular music, and I just couldn't get a thing out of it. My heart wasn't in it.

We'd go out to some bar, and sometimes, if it was a country band playing, we would enjoy ourselves. The larger portion of the people were country people and they'd get all dressed up and come and listen to the music and dance all night. There were a few who couldn't handle the booze and would start a fight. . . . I imagine it was just too frustrating to try to cope with the new way that they were living. And there was a bar on every corner.

. . . How *could* they have been prepared for what they would encounter when they moved to the city?

—HAZEL DICKENS

David Gahr

70

When I went up North, the first thing that happened was that I started drinking about twice as heavy as I ever had before in my life. It was a form of recreation. I had nothing to do. The way I was brought up, when I wanted to have some fun I'd pick up my dog and I'd go hunting or I'd go fishing. There always was a lot of land around. . . .

When I got up North, all of a sudden I was in a totally different situation. I tried to replace hunting and fishing with drinking and shooting pool.

There was also this whole sort of machismo thing that builds up in men that have been robbed of their masculinity. The only way I had to express myself as a man was to knock somebody's head off his shoulders. I couldn't express myself in the ways society tells me I ought to—which is buy a color TV set for my family (and me making $1.15 an hour). I could express myself in the way my surroundings told me I could—which was knock somebody's block off.

The mountains ain't no picnic; they're rough too. But it's not like it is up North. It's not as vicious. I fought some in the mountains too, but it wasn't the same. It wasn't so ingrained.

—JOHN ARMS

Uptown has been called a port of entry. There are a lot of southern people living in Chicago. And when you come up, you're coming into a community of people.

I have real strong feelings about the migration thing because I live in an area of Chicago where a lot of people come who are driven off the land. I know there are kids up there whose feet's never walked on anything but concrete. And I know people who have been caught in the cycles of poverty, if you want to be poetic about it. But it's not very poetic if you live in some of those situations.

I'm not an economist, but I feel that the economic decisions that have been made lately are going to drive more people from rural areas, and into industrial areas. We're going to have to be prepared for that and, if possible, be in a position to influence those decisions.

—DOUG YOUNGBLOOD

The bars are one of the social gathering places in the city. The church is not as strong as it is in the South. There's not that much opportunity for the kinds of religion we learn in the South. When you get off from work, you head right for one of the hillbilly bars, where you're among your own people and you feel free and you don't have to worry about how your voice sounds, how you're dressing.

—DOUG YOUNGBLOOD

UPTOWN CHICAGO KIND OF BLUES

WORDS AND MUSIC: DOUG YOUNGBLOOD

I ___ watch the child-ren play___ing in___ the pud-dles__ left__ by__ rain___ Un-der-neath the el-tracks, in the noise of a train; But the chil-dren___ of the wealth___y lack no-thing for their games, As I ___ stare ___ at this un – fair-ness, Fin-gers of fire_____ Keep a – reach-ing for__ my brain.

I watch the children playing in the puddles left by rain
Underneath the el-tracks, in the noise of a train;
But the children of the wealthy lack nothing for their games,
As I stare at this unfairness,
Fingers of fire
Keep a-reaching for my brain.

Oh, the times are gettin' better you'll hear the rich explain
But our lives are never different 'cause nothin's ever changed
Oh, it's us who do the labor but the wealth is in their name
As I see this selfishness,
Fingers of fire
Keep a-reaching for my brain.

I see the prison filling with my people and I explain
We all want the good life, yeah, we all want the same.
But unequal distribution makes that impossible to gain.
As I see the contradictions,
Fingers of fire
Keep a-reaching for my brain.

And the teachers and the preachers, yeah, they all do explain;
Suffer here on earth and in heaven lay your claim.
While they feast upon our harvest and drink of our champagne.
When I see their well-fed faces,
Fingers of fire
Keep a-reaching for my brain.

Now you who rule us with pistols and moneyed chains
There's gonna be a difference 'cause we're gonna rearrange
All that you've erected made of hunger, hate and pain.
Yeah, we're gonna stop
Fingers of fire
From a-reaching for our brains.

BLUE RIDGE MOUNTAIN REFUGEE

WORDS AND MUSIC: SI AND KATHY KAHN

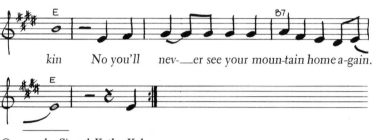

I'm work—ing in a ____ fac-to-ry ____ and

think—ing how it ____ feels To be ____

bring-ing home good mon-ey ____ like my Dad—dy ne–ver

seen But a ____ feel-ing fol-lows ____ af—ter me like a

hound dog at my _____ _____ 'Cause I ____

know that I'll ne-ver see ____ my moun–tain home a-gain.

____ Oh they say that ____ you can't go home a—gain ____

Nev-er ____ set ____ and talk ____ a-mong your child-hood

friends Nev-er ____ live ____ a-mong your neigh-bors and your

kin No you'll nev—er see your moun-tain home a-gain.

I'm working in a factory and thinking how it feels
To be bringing home good money like my Daddy never seen
But a feeling follows after me like a hound dog at my heels
'Cause I know that I'll never see my mountain home again.

> Oh they say that you can't go home again
> Never set and talk among your childhood friends
> Never live among your neighbors and your kin
> No you'll never see your mountain home again.

Down at the railway station in the early afternoon
You can see them carrying bundles that are all done up in twine
And they hear the whistle from the south, they're saying their
    goodbyes
And they say they'll be back, but they're leaving for all time.

> Don't they know that you can't go home again
> Never set and talk among your childhood friends
> Never live among your neighbors and your kin
> No they'll never see their mountain homes again.

In Cincinnati, Baltimore, Chicago and Detroit
You will find us by the thousands with our husbands and our wives
If you wonder what we're doing here so far from our mountain homes
We're Blue Ridge Mountain refugees, fighting for our lives.

> And we know that we can't go home again
> Never set and talk among our childhood friends
> Never live among our neighbors and our kin
> No we'll never see our mountain homes again.

I was born and raised there, in West Virginia. I like the place very well, but it's just come to where you can't make anything to live on, see. That's the reason why I don't want to go back. When them mines were all goin and everybody had jobs, why, you could get a hold a somethin then, you know, to live on. But now, you see, there's so many on relief that you can go into that relief office and Lord, it'll take you a week or so to get signed up on relief. Then they gonna give you a bawlin out, say you gotta do somethin.

—RAS BRYANT

Young migrant family in Uptown Chicago

Danny Lyon, Magnum Photos

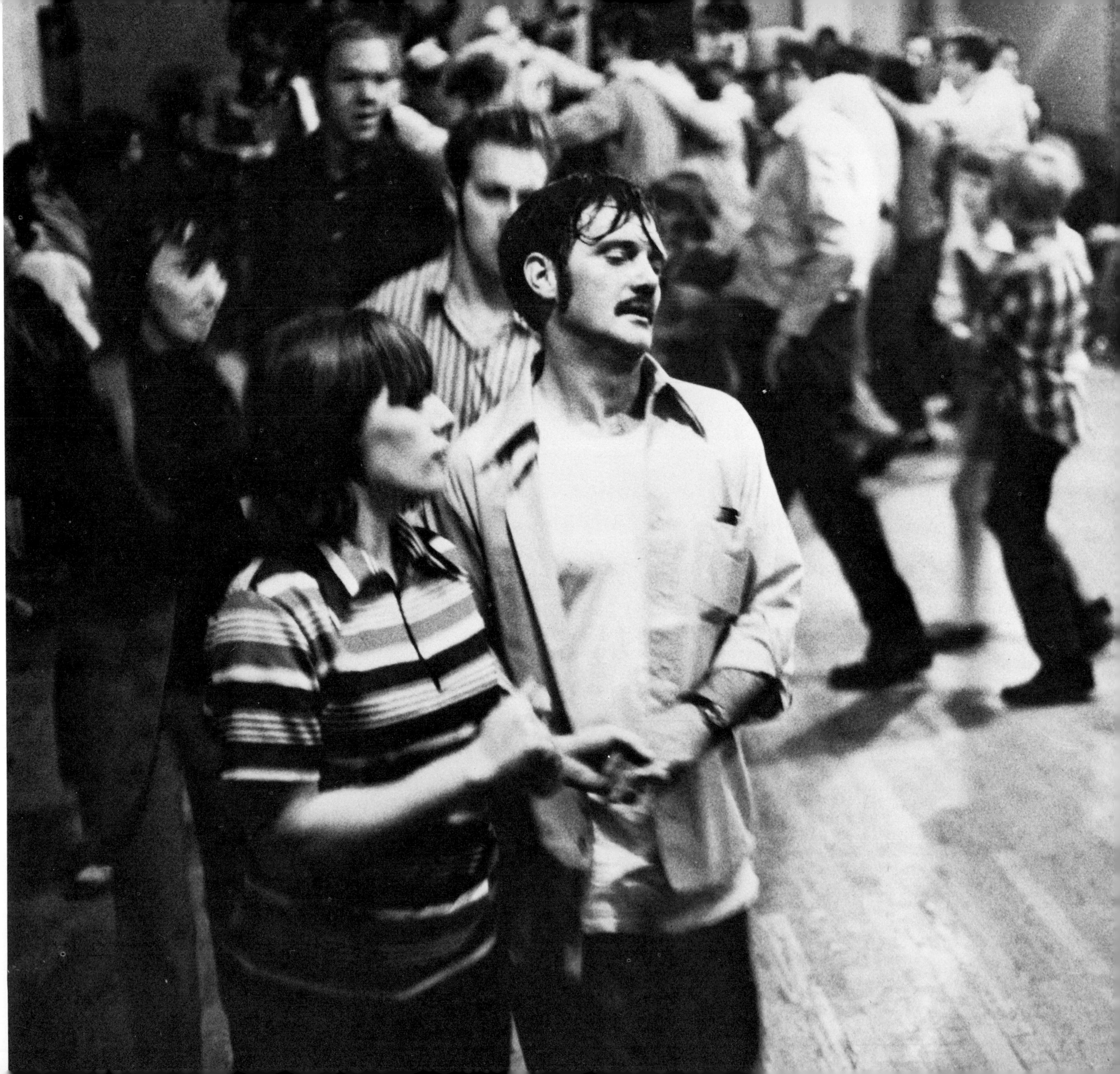
Phil Primack

I left the mountains of Letcher County in 1955, two weeks after graduation from high school. My reason for leaving was like that of so many thousands of others before me, to find employment and a better way of life.

Of all the people who graduated with me, I know of only three who are still in Letcher County. The rest of us are in Ohio, Michigan, and California. We followed the graduating classes before us, and we were followed by the graduating classes of succeeding years.

We all left Letcher County for the same reason: to find work. We have bought cars, homes and real estate in our new state. We no longer vote in Kentucky, nor do we pay taxes there. But being native-born "Briars," we can't get Kentucky out of our blood. Everytime I meet another person from Letcher County, one question is always asked, "When was the last time you was down *home?*"

I would venture to say that if enough work was available in Letcher County, 90% of us would come home.

—JIM CORNETT

I celebrate the fact that this Appalachia has a hold on me. Wherever I go, I'm of these hills. That little cabin at the head of the holler has been in the back of my mind, like an anchor with a long rope, all the time I've been having to make a home for my family elsewhere—and someday soon I mean to build that cabin, because here is where I belong. No one has to tell me that—I know.

—JEAN RITCHIE

LAST OLD TRAIN'S A-LEAVIN'

WORDS AND MUSIC: JEAN RITCHIE

Standin' on the mountain, standin' on the mountain,
Standin' on the mountain, don't you want to go?
    O the last old train's a-leavin', the last old train's a-leavin',
    The last old train's a-leavin', don't you want to go?

Hear the hills a-falling, hear the hills a-falling,
Hear the hills a-falling, don't you want to go?
Hear the nightbirds calling, hear the nightbirds calling,
Hear the nightbirds calling, I don't want to go!
    O the last old train's a-leavin', etc.

See the timber burning, see the timber burning,
See the timber burning, don't you want to go?
See my newground turning, see my newground turning,
See my newground turning, I don't want to go!
    O the last old train's a-leavin', etc.

See the people going, see the people going,
See the people going, don't you want to go?
See my redbuds glowing, see my redbuds glowing,
See my redbuds glowing, I don't want to go!
    O the last old train's a-leavin', etc.

Standin' on the mountain, standin' on the mountain,
Standin' on the mountain, don't you want to go?
    O the last old train's a-leavin', etc.

79

III. TALKING COMMUNITY ACTION BLUES

The War on Poverty

...The poor people lost the War on Poverty. Congress forced them to lose it. They don't want poor people to organize and they don't aim for them to organize.
But until they do organize, they'll never do no good.

—EVERETTE THARP

Kenneth Murray © 1970

An $18-a-day vacation in Mingo County, West Virginia—
land of the Hatfields and McCoys. See and learn first-hand
the problems of the poor by living with a mountain family.
Become involved in Appalachian culture. Ideal for the in-
tellect who wishes to learn.

—ad in The New Republic

DISCOVERED AGAIN . . .

Each time we are "discovered," a passel of new missionaries
invade the mountains. Old clothes, surplus food and such are
made available and some temporary reforms may result—
crumbs thrown to the poor who need whole loaves and some
meat, too. Some stirring is stimulated. Hope flutters pain-
fully to escape the lint covered mill-hills or dust blackened
shacks behind slate dumps only to fall broken-winged in
polluted air or rivers outside. The missionary effect is to dull
the razor-edge thrust of the people toward human better-
ment. Appalachia's colonial status is left in tact, hardly
shaken or questioned.

Southern Appalachia is a colonial possession of Eastern
based industry. Like all exploited colonial areas, the "mother
country" may make generous gestures now and then, send
missionaries with up-lift programs, "superior" religion, build
churches and sometimes schools. They'll do about everything
—except get off the backs of the people, end the exploitive
domination. . . .

. . . There is a lesson to be learned from all these outside efforts that have failed to save us. If we native mountaineers can now determine to organize and save ourselves, save our mountains from the spoilers who tear them down, pollute our streams and leave grotesque areas of ugliness, there is hope.

It is time that we hill folk should understand and appreciate our heritage, stand up like those who were our ancestors, develop our own self-identity. It is time to realize that nobody from the outside is ever going to save us from bad conditions unless we make our own stand. We must learn to organize again, speak, plan and act for ourselves. There are many potential allies with common problems— the poor of the great cities, the Indians, the blacks who are also exploited. They need us. We need them. Solidarity is still crucial. If we learn this lesson from the outside "missionary" failures, then we are on our way.

—DON WEST

Earl Dotter

Anything less than

> —hydroelectric power facilities to provide cheap electric power for our cities, towns and industry;
>
> —adequate highways throughout Appalachia;
>
> —appropriate federal safeguards against the ravages of strip mining;
>
> —a program of reforestation and soil conservation;
>
> —strict enforcement of our civil liberties as guaranteed to us by the Constitution of the United States; and
>
> —the reassertion of our right to organize and bargain collectively

will not measure up to a true war on poverty.

—EVERETTE THARP

The VISTA workers and outsiders that come in here. All they ever talk about is white paint for our schools and cultural enrichment for our children in the community. But if we don't do something about the bulldozers stripping the head of this creek, we ain't going to have no community or kids, either one. . . .

—from the album notes
of "The Poverty War Is Dead,"
by MICHAEL KLINE

TALKING COMMUNITY ACTION BLUES

WORDS: MICHAEL KLINE

If you want a better life, let me tell you what to do
You gotta talk to the boys on the creek with you
Build up your community and make it strong
And if you all work together boys, it won't take long
To get
    Better roads, white paint on your schools, happiness in future
      years,
    Appalachian Volunteers, incorporated.

Now some folks find it hard to see
Just why you got to build up your community
But I think it'll work and let me tell you why
Better times is comin', it's in the sky
We'll have
    An end to war, an end to ignorance, an end to sorriness,
    An end to prejudice and won't that be nice?

Now maybe you come up when times was hard
And you counted it a blessing to have cold biscuits and lard
You didn't have doctors and roads and such
And you got along, boys, without having too much
You made it.
    Every year though they told you times was gonna get better,
    Every election year! They told ya!

And then back since the days of wagons and horses
Outside folks been stealin' your natural resources
They cut down the timber, like men that was mad
And stripped your land of all the value it had
They called it
    The industrial revolution, looked more to me like stream and
    River pollution.

'Course the people was happy while the jobs held out
There was times of plenty 'midst the times of drought
When automation took away the work of hands
Young folks began to leave these Appalachian lands
Headed out
    For Dayton, Cincinnati, Chicago town
    Huntin' work, finding hardship all around.

But now it's the year 1966
And all over this country folks are having their kicks
People makin' good all over the nation
Prosperity set by the corporations
They're the big boys
    Organized, they control the mines and steel and price increases,
    If you let 'em, they'd control you, your nephews and your nieces.

And you'd work from dawn to dark without regard to age
And you're barely makin' starvation wages
So you talk to the judge and he'd never tell
But before he'd see you richer boys, he'd see you in hell
He's a slick-'un
    Got him a self-interested gut and he'll always get along on
    His boot-leg cut.

Or if you can't find work, they call you fools
And they put you on the "Pappies" but don't give you any tools
Readin' and writin' comes every other night
And they teach you you're not supposed to think or fight
Just take it easy, boys
Big Daddy, the county judge, knows what's best,
Go easy, boys, and get plenty of rest.

Well now boys, I'm singing an angry song
And I could sing it all night but it would take too long
So let me give you some examples what I'm talkin' about
And I know you'll be able to figure it out.
    On Bloody Creek they hadn't had a road for years
    So they got 'em some Ohio volunteers
    They gleaned rocks from the hills, so I am told
    And they made rocky patches on their gutted out roads.
    College kids . . . hard workers . . . pretty singers . . . 9 lb.
        hammer swingers.

Down in Barwick they had a little different style
You see they didn't have a truck or tools or tiles
So they got 'em some paint, and with hands just a few
They fixed up the school 'til it looked like new
It's a slow beginnin' . . . workin' without tools, but you try to tell
  me
Them guys in Barwick is fools.

And up at Myer's Fork they thought they'd give it a whirl
With a brand new Vista, dolly girl
She proved to be tough and a tolerable raider
And all workin' together they stole a county grader
It took three, four to pick it up out of the sand
Where the county judge had left it stand.

But they got it back home, they rolled for the grade
And by the end of the week the boys had learned 'em a trade
They called it Heavy Equipment
Now they're waitin' for a shipment all their own.

You see the Federal Government through Uncle Sam
They're the boys who put the power line in the electric dam
They've talked it over and 'bout half agreed
It's gonna have to be up to you and me
It's called the war on poverty
Maximized feasible participation of the culturally deprived
Low-income target group
Lord have mercy, I wonder when they're gonna get a start on poor
    people.

You'll find community work full of heartbreaks and joys
And every now and then you have to make a little noise
But when conflict comes with the other side
Let 'em know you'll not be the ones to go and hide
Talk it over boys, speak your mind, incorporate,
And then stipulate.

Well now boys, you've come to the hardest job
Cause that OEO's about a fussed-up mob
They read Sociology and a little folk lore
And they call each other experts on the Appalachian poor
They fool around with project designs
Play with people's futures, bodies and minds
But when it comes to deliverin' the goods
You find 'em all heading fer the deep, dark woods
    Scared, sensitive, high-salaried bureaucrats, embers-members.

Now I could go on and tell you a whole lot more
'Bout how the C.A.P. has failed to reach the poor
I might make you mad, but I'd mean you no harm
If I's to tell you 'bout the poor folks down on Turner's farm
Hard times in the country
    Winter winds howlin', empty bellies of poor, hungry younguns
    Growlin'.

But it's enough to say that on Turner's Creek
And wherever folks are provin' they're not so weak
At the UK campus and the Cumberland school
And wherever A.V.s are playin' it cool
In Hurricane, Verda, Pittytown and Ligon
And wherever folks are fightin', sweatin' and diggin'
I'm sure they'll all tell you with satisfaction,
Boys, you oughta get a piece of that community action.
No sir
    You can't eat it; but by God brother,
    It's hard to beat it.

© 1969 by Michael Kline

Photo by Robert Cooper © 1972

I remember one day I was sitting on my porch, just minding my own business. I hadn't done nothin' to nobody that day. This VISTA come jogging up in a sweat suit. He waved, and I waved back. That was my fatal mistake. He turned in the driveway and jogged up to the porch. He proceeded to tell me about the VISTA program and finally invited me to go swimming the next day.

So I went swimming, and some of my buddies went swimming, and we got to talking about education. And I was real interested, because I was having some trouble in school myself right then. I didn't know what was wrong—I didn't know specifics—but I knew something was wrong. I had that much sense.

Anyway, I got involved, and I progressed really fast until I was working for the War on Poverty. And I really thought that I could use that vehicle to do some good things in the community, things I thought ought to be done. But as I got into it, I began to discover things—like the director was paid $23,000 a year. And they were complaining because I was turning in $100 a month mileage and travel expenses. They didn't have money to pay back community people for actual expenses they had in trying to organize people, and yet they could pay an administrator $23,000 a year. One third of the OEO budget in these programs went for administration. . . .

I began to realize something else about the poverty program. As soon as you began to get good and get something going, they dropped you like a hot potato. In actuality, it was nothing more than something to buy up people's energy. So I decided to quit. I went north and got a job.

I found out pretty quick that wasn't for me either and came back home. I was laying around for a while not doing anything, when I remembered that there were guys in the poverty program getting $23,000 for doing the same thing. Why couldn't I get a piece of the action? I did a lot of volunteer time; I'll just count it as back pay. So I got a job with a poverty agency, and I was out for a hustle.

I was making a pretty decent wage—more money than I ever made in my life, doing less than I ever had in my life. As a matter of fact, the less I did, the happier they were. But the thing that was happening, that finally got me, was that they were using me. I thought I was using them; but they were writing up, and getting, $50,000 programs off the fact that I was working for them. No longer was I just "John Arms from halfway up Stephen's Branch Hollow" . . . I was "John Arms, Superorganizer," made over into the image of these people that considered themselves our saviors. I saw my own people as they saw them—apathetic, incapable of figuring things out for themselves. That's what kills me most about intellectuals and professionals. They will go to their graves never admitting that I have a mind and that I, too, can think. They will not recognize the fact that poor people are capable of their own thoughts.

Usually the older people were established in their identity, and they didn't suffer as much as the young people did. I don't know of a single individual under twenty-five years old who became involved extensively with the poverty war that didn't in some way, shape, or form lose part of his identity. Some regained it later, and some never have.

—JOHN ARMS

89

On the "happy pappy" program we dug graves, cut weeds, fit fires, built swinging bridges, did all kind of things. It was officially called the "Work Experience and Training Program." You had to go to school one day a week. To be eligible you had to be unemployed and have one or more children.

They were always trying to get you off of it and put you into some kind of training for electronics or something or other which you knew you'd never get a job in eastern Kentucky. Nobody'd ever fall for it. Mountain people aren't that dumb. They just hung on to what they had, and I don't blame them. The $1.25 an hour was a sure thing.

If they were going to spend all that money, why didn't they spend it on something that would help us—some kind of training work, heavy equipment, welding, auto mechanics?

—BUCK MAGGARD

I think we all went into the War on Poverty with a lot of hopes. I got into it by accident.

We were fighting fire on the "happy pappy" program. That's one of the hardest darn jobs you'll ever get tangled up with. .

We'd fit fire for sixteen hours straight. We'd fought two fires that day and 'long about ten at night we still hadn't had supper; we'd had no rest. We were dead tired. And they had us way up on the south fork of Quicksand. I was so tired I couldn't hardly get out of the truck.

I just told 'em, "I can't do anything else today; sixteen hours a day is all you can work us." (I don't know where I got that, but somewhere along the way I'd heard that after so many hours you had to give a man a break; give him something to eat.) I said, "I'm gonna take a break. I haven't had nothing to eat and I'm tired." I said, "I'm not going to fight any more fire tonight."

They said, "You have to."

I said, "No, we don't have to, now. You can't make us."

Well, when I refused to go, there was another guy refused to go. And then before I know it, there was six of us refused to go out of about twelve of us and two fire bosses. One of 'em had a gun on and the other one had a carbine in his truck. So five more stepped over and said, "We're not going either." Said, "You're gonna have to take us home."

They said, "We won't take you home."

We said, "That's all right, we'll walk."

They didn't think we'd do it. This old fire warden he jerked his pistol out and shot it into the ground trying to scare us. And none of us didn't move. Then he come up to this big, tall feller and punched him in the gut with the gun and pulled the trigger. It snapped but luckily it didn't fire. I don't know if he'd shot all the shells out or it was an act of God or what, but anyway he's still livin'.

But when he done that, that just made us all so much madder we just said, "We're goin'." And we took off a-walkin'.

We were still walkin' when daylight come. And they had gotten scared by this time by what was happening. They knew their jobs were in jeopardy if we really made a stink about it, so they come off the job and run us down and tried to give us rides into Jackson.

We refused to ride with 'em. And that scared 'em that much more. We knew we had the upper hand so we stuck together. . . .

We finally got into Jackson, we went right on into the office. We didn't stop nowhere. Some old smart-aleck woman was in there, said, "What are you all doin' in here?"

We said, "That's a good question, lady. We've come in here to see the likes of you all."

She said, "What can we do for you this morning?"

We said, "You can't do nothin' for us. We want to see the big woman." (That was Barbara Turner, who was the head of the thing.) "We don't even want to talk to you . . . we want to see Barbara." So we just barged on in there. And

Coal miner Francis Pikitus

we told her what was happening; how the men were being treated and all.

Of course they said, "We'll do something about that." And of course they did. I never got to work with any of those five men again.

I got put in the county judge's office. When I got put in there I really began to see how things were working. I began to get an insight into things I'd heard rumors about, but didn't really care about. But there I began to see it right before my own eyes. And from that, I began to talk to other people around in communities, and we finally got this little group going called the Grassroots Citizens Committee. And I was made the first chairman of it.

We began to put out a little community newspaper—me and my brother put it out for about a year—called the *Grassroots Gossip*.

And that's how I got into the whole thing. We started out with the basic little things like how the men were being treated on the "happy pappy" jobs, and the conditions of the schools, roads, stuff like that. Nothin' really dramatic, just basic stuff.

—BUCK MAGGARD

Earl Dotter

*Joe Mulloy, Appalachian Volunteer
from Kentucky*

During the poverty war, when us professional poor people . . . were in such demand, . . . you could get $50 a day just for going to a conference and sitting there so everybody could see you. Maybe you wouldn't have to say more than five or six words—just let them know you were there. And then they could spend the rest of the day interpreting what you said.

So I came up with the idea of "Arms' Rent-a-Token Agency." For a fee, we can send you for your conference just any representative from any organization you want. It would really save the people putting on these conferences all the trouble of going out and finding their own token, because we'd have this umbrella organization. We'd have a catalogue —by interest, race, sex. We could give you a "black Appalachian militant coal miner." Of course, he'd be rather expensive because they're pretty hard to come by. But for the right price we might even be able to come up with a "black Appalachian militant coal miner who plays the banjo." Or if your tastes are more simple, we could just give you a white mountain guy who's concerned about strip mining. You can find a lot of them. It's all based on supply and demand. The scarcer the token wanted, the higher the price.

—JOHN ARMS

People were living on mountain greens and corn meal when the poverty war came in. It did feed a lot of people. It got medical services to a lot of people. But like Joe Begley says, "It's like trying to treat a cancer with an aspirin."

Poor people are not poor because they don't have roads and doctors and clothes. Poor people are poor because they don't have money. If I have money, I can get my own doctor, my own clothes, my own medical care. So why not invest the money in something that's gonna produce safe, humane jobs? If they were worried about the economic condition of the people in eastern Kentucky at that time, then why didn't they create an economy in a region where there was none—no jobs, no money, no nothin'? Instead they got into this charity thing. Nothing is more degrading to the mountain man who's been raised to take care of himself.

—JOHN ARMS

Earl Dotter

When we started, the organizations were really controlled by the poor people. And this is what Congress got scared of . . . poor people controlling all that federal money. So that's when Carl Perkins got to work and got Edith Green to sponsor an amendment which took the power out of the hands of the poor people and gave it to the local officials.

Then people began to see how the government moves to kill stuff when something starts to happen. There was a lot of stuff going on and the government was moving all the time to stop it. And if that doesn't work, they could cut the funds off. It was just that simple.

—BUCK MAGGARD

The courthouse bunch was the first to organize groups "acceptable" to the Government. They picked up their pencils and filled out the forms in the back rooms of courthouses and schoolboard offices. And the poverty millions were channeled into them and their kin.

The schoolboard and the health department and the county court which had already failed to provide mountain people with education, health and justice were given control of the poverty war by the bureaucrats and specialists in Washington.

—MICHAEL KLINE

OUT AT THE COURTHOUSE

WORDS AND MUSIC: BILL CHRISTOPHER

Out at the court-house where things__ are__ go-ing on,__

__ Where__ lit-tle old shad-y deals__ are made, they

real-ly__ mean no wrong.__ Pick up__ a

dol-lar here and__ there they got to get__ a-long__

__ Out at the court-house where

things are go-ing on.

© 1975 by Bill Christopher

Out at the courthouse where things are going on,
Where little old shady deals are made, they really mean no wrong.
Pick up a dollar here and there—they got to get along
Out at the courthouse where things are going on.

We got the nicest, finest judge although he likes his wine.
They say he's really quite a card when he's feeling fine.
But when he gets to stepping high, he can't stand alone
Out at the courthouse where things are going on.

They say my tax is mighty low, that it's just and fair,
And I guess I'm really proud that I can pay my share.
All the folks that know the man must have a broken heart
To realize that they alone don't get to pay their part.

Out at the courthouse where things are going on,
Where little old shady deals are made, they really mean no wrong.
Pick up a dollar here and there—they got to get along
Out at the courthouse where things are going on.

Election day has come and gone and all the bad guys lost.
All the good guys out there say they're cutting down on costs.
I guess they are, it must be me, 'cause some call me a fool—
Our roads are full of bumps and holes and they just closed our school.

In our nation's Congress they know their way around,
They know how to wheel and deal as all you folks have found.
But out at the courthouse such things are going on,
Should D.C. see these things we see, you'd hear them sing this song:

Out at the courthouse where things are going on,
Where little old shady deals are made, they really mean no wrong.
Pick up a dollar here and there—they got to get along
Out at the courthouse,
Out at the courthouse where things are going on.

GO TELL SARGENT SHRIVER

WORDS: MICHAEL KLINE
MUSIC: "GO TELL AUNT RHODY"

Go tell Sargent Shriver,
Go tell Robert McNamara,
Go tell Lyndon Johnson,
That the poverty war is dead.

The one that they've been saving on,
The one that we've been slaving on,
The one that they've been economizing on
To feather their pretty heads.

It died in the Congress,
It died in the Congress,
It died in the Congress
Because it was painted red.
    Go tell Sargent Shriver, etc.

The politicians are lying,
Our boys in Vietnam are dying,
The Great Society's crying
Because its children won't be fed.
    Go tell Sargent Shriver, etc.

The president has washed his hands,
We've got commitments, boys, in Asian lands,
The government has other plans
To build bombs and planes instead.
    Go tell Sargent Shriver, etc.

© 1969 by Michael Kline (words)

Madeline James speaks out at congressional hearing in Washington, D.C., November, 1971.

Mike Knapik

Mike Knapik

Bertha Allen forces Senator John Sherman Cooper to return to a meeting between Appalachians and their Representatives.

. . . After the people began to organize in city ghettos and in mountain hollows and creeks, the establishment became scared all over the United States—the mayors in all the big cities got scared. They didn't want the poor people to organize. So they prevailed upon Congress to change the law. And Congress did change the law. They put poor people out of the boards, or as good as put them out. They left a mere handful in to discuss the problems and things, but they had no power. They gave the power to the politicians—the county judges and the county officials. They gave it back to the establishment and they done as they pleased; they hired who they pleased. They hired people that was wealthy instead of poor. The poverty program's become state and federal agencies.

So the poor people lost the War on Poverty. Congress forced them to lose it. They still today don't want poor people to organize, and they don't aim for them to organize. But until they do organize, they'll never do no good.

—EVERETTE THARP

Letha Woods and Eula Hall, from east Kentucky

The poverty war died quickly. Most of the OEO agencies came under the control of local politicians, but many of the community leaders who originally became active in OEO programs went on to form welfare rights organizations, lobby for black lung benefits, oppose strip mining, create cooperatives and health clinics, and investigate school problems. Through their early struggles many of them have become tough and knowledgeable and have developed a long-range perspective on political power and how it can be wrestled from the hands of established political machines.

—MIKE CLARK

I got into welfare rights through a school-lunch program. We found out that the domination we were under was something the local officials had thought up. It was not in the law books. So we started fighting back. And we've accomplished quite a bit. When you see someone who's been held under the Welfare Department's thumb for years get up and walk into the Welfare Commissioner's office and tell him off, that's progress.

People are beginning to wake up to the fact that those guys are in there to do a job for *me*; what am I afraid of them for? I'm not their slave; they're supposed to be working for me.

—SHELVA THOMPSON

Mike Clark

EKWRO [East Kentucky Welfare Rights Organization] started with a school-lunch program. We had a new school built in our area with a modern lunchroom. But the kids that couldn't pay couldn't eat. . . . The only kids that could afford to buy lunch would be the teacher's kids or a coal operator's kids. And most of the poor people had to hear from their kids every day that they were forced to sit on the stage and watch the kids that had a quarter eat. . . . That was the beginning of our welfare-rights group. Within a month we had a hundred members and we wound up having a march on Prestonsburg and an all-out battle with the county superintendent. We won the issue and we did get free and reduced lunches for the children.

And it taught people something. They said, "Well, if we can get a school-lunch program as effective as this, we can straighten out the P.A. [Public Assistance] office, the Food Stamp office. In fact we'll just take on anything that we think ain't right." So from there on we've been battling with coal operators and politicians and doctors.

Another battle that the welfare-rights group won was about the comprehensive health care program that we had in Floyd County. . . . The politicians and doctors and the bigwigs were getting all the money and the people were getting little or no service. It took a while, but the welfare-rights group was successful in getting that program defunded.

Now we have our own clinic which is not funded by anybody. It's self-supporting. We have two good doctors and people's treated . . . that can't pay. I think the welfare-rights group's come a long way.

—EULA HALL

Shelva Thompson tells Senators, Congressmen, and their aides about pitfalls in planned welfare legislation during the Survival March on Washington, November, 1971.

I think the worst conception that people have is that welfare is some kind of a charity organization that is there to help the poor, lazy bum who doesn't want to work. They should know that welfare was not established until a few hundred out-of-work and disabled coal miners camped on the Capitol lawn, demanding some kind of benefits that they could feed their families on. They'd been crippled and butchered in the coal mines; they'd been cut out of work; and they had nothing to live on. That's the way welfare got started. Too many people think that welfare is something that was set up by the government to help people. It wasn't. It was fought for, and won by the people.

—SHELVA THOMPSON

Edith and Jake Easterling,
Poorbottom, Kentucky

I think people learned a lot from the War on Poverty. I know I did. I had so many shocking things happen to me during that time, part of it seems like a dream.

I well remember the first time Joe Mulloy came and talked to me about strip mining. At that time everybody was whispering about how they didn't like it. I told him how I felt about it, but I said people really won't say anything. He said, "That's the point, Edith. You've got to speak out and say what you think." And I thought, "Lord, no . . . they'd put you in jail. You could never speak out."

And then so many things happened. When the severence tax came up I thought, "We'll never get that off of these coal operators." And when we went through so much on the black lung fight I felt, "Well, we're hammering on this, but we'll never get it." When we did, it gave me confidence, made me feel, "Well, you *can*, if you holler long enough about these things."

—EDITH EASTERLING

IV. COME ALL YOU COAL MINERS
Early Days in the Mines

I began working in the mines when I was only thirteen years old. In those days we had a child-labor law, but the way the companies evaded this was to not have a boy on the payroll. But they would turn his time in to his father. So my father was a-drawing my pay, but I was supposed to be getting it. Then if I should have got killed in the mines, why the company would say, "No, we had no such boy on the payroll."
When I first started, I was a trapper. I worked for 10 cents an hour and I worked ten hours a day for 60 cents.

—TILLMAN CADLE

My father worked in the mines—going in before daylight, coming out after dark. I hardly ever seen my old man till after the United Mine Workers organized in 1934. He practically seemed like a strange man to me because he was out working and slaving for us.

—GEORGE TUCKER

106

CLAY COUNTY MINER

WORDS AND MUSIC: HAZEL DICKENS

He's a poor man 'cause mining's all he's known
And miners don't get rich loading coal
He's a sick man 'cause that coal dust took its stand
But he don't expect to get no help from that operator man.
  Well it's good-bye Old Timer, I guess our time has come
  Those water holes, that dirty coal dust eating up our lungs
  We'll leave this world just as poor as the day we saw the sun
  Well it's good-bye Old Timer, all our mining is done.

I remember the time when I could load more coal than any man
Now my health is gone, buried in down in that dirty ground
And they've taken away my rights, privilege to be a man
But I know that I can't tell all that to that operator man.
  Well it's good-bye Old Timer, etc.

Remember Old Timer, when we were little kids
When we'd talk about our mining days when we'd get grown and big
But now we're old, broken men, they don't need us around
Though we gave our lives to make them rich, they won't give us a
  dime.
  Well it's good-bye Old Timer, etc.

A mine may go 5 and 6 miles back into a mountain. It may take as long as thirty minutes on a mantrip [a car which carries the miners through the mine], and even then it may be another mile or mile and a half of walking for a miner to get to his room or place of work.

Most of the time you walked on your knees. I spent most of my time in 36-inch coal. We'd tie our cable on, go back 125 feet behind somethin' or another, touch a shot off, and come back and hook another one on. And go back in. It took at least three shots to shoot one cut. Most of the time it took five. . . . You could see the smoke and flames come out of the room 75 to 100 feet.

You get out of breath in there and there wasn't no air, but you still breathe somethin', so you sucked that dust and the fumes from that powder. And Law', it was awful.

—JAKE EASTERLING

We was bein' told to do whatever the company and bosses told us to do, regardless of what hardships it was—goin' in water holes and standin' in water to our knees to load coal. You'd shovel more water than you would coal.

I've come home many a night in the wintertime, way after dark, come in with my clothes froze so stiff my clothes would stand up. They'd done eat supper and all gone to bed and my old mother'd hear me go by and she'd say, "There's poor little Jim—listen to his clothes rub together, froze stiff." If you'd forget and pull your cap off too quick, it would pull your hair out—be frozen to your hair.

It was just a way of making people be slaves, because they had to do that to live.

But we done it, didn't we, brother Jake?

—JIM HAMILTON

Kenneth Murray © 1970

The only thing about a coal miner. He don't have a chance to enjoy life. When the spring time comes and the grass gets about that high, the birds are singing, buddy, I'd druther take a beating as to go to work, but yet I would take a whipping as to not work, too. You know I want to work but I like to be outside, listen to the birds sing. In the coal mine all you see is a few old rats running around now and then, and you have to follow a light all the time to see. You can't enjoy that too well, you know.

—JIM JACKSON

Coal sometimes lies in narrow seams, often less than three feet thick. A man must lie on his side or crawl on his belly to work in seams like that. To sit up is difficult, to stand is impossible.

. . . Every job in the mines was dangerous. There was hardly any room for men operating equipment to maneuver their machines, and there was not enough space above the machinery to see where they were going. The noise of drilling and undercutting coal and blasting it loose seemed twice as deafening as in a mine with more standing room. Dust swirled through the dark passages and settled on everything: machines, hands, faces, nostrils, eyelids. And whatever else you could do, you could not stand up to stretch, no matter how much you wanted to. And if something happened—if you heard the roof of the mine "working" over your head and knew it was going to fall, or if there were an explosion— you knew there was no way you could run to the surface, because there was not enough headroom anywhere. You could only crawl.

—THOMAS N. BETHELL

110

THIRTY INCH COAL

WORDS AND MUSIC: MIKE PAXTON
AS SUNG BY GEORGE TUCKER

Grab a pick and sho-vel__, bring your safe-ty__ light

Don't for-get your fu-ses and your dy-na-mite

Put on__ your knee-pads__ and your safe-ty-toes

We're going to the coal-mine where the coal is low.

Ri-din' on a li__zard in the thir-ty inch coal

See the cab-le spark-lin', watch the lit-tle wheels roll

Now Lord have mer-cy__ on a mi-ner's__ soul

Down on your poor knees in the thir-ty inch coal.

2.

Grab a pick and shovel, bring your safety light
Don't forget your fuses and your dynamite
Put on your knee-pads and your safety-toes
We're going to the coal mine where the coal is low.
    Ridin' on a lizard in the thirty inch coal
    See the cable sparklin', watch the little wheels roll
    Now Lord have mercy on a miner's soul
    Down on your poor knees in the thirty inch coal.

Timber up that heading, set the wedges tight
Or your wife and your children won't see you tonight
Spread out a little rock dust, spread a little bit more
To keep that coal dust on the mining floor.
    Ridin' on a lizard, etc.*

* Alternative verses and chorus by Mike Paxton:

Make a brattice yonder, make a brattice there
Gotta give the miner a little breathin' air
Spread around that rock dust, spread a little more
Keep that fiery coal dust smothered on the floor.
    Ridin' on a lizard in the thirty inch coal
    Drag-cable a-sparkin' as the little wheels roll
    Workin' like a beaver, diggin' like a mole
    Down on my knees in the thirty inch coal.

Timber up that heading, make the wedges tight
Or your wife and children won't see you tonight
Waiting is that mountain, as it's always been
Waiting is that mountain that swallowed up your kin.
    Ridin' on a lizard, etc.

111

I remember the days when my boy would follow me to the coal mine. I had to take him back home. I began to think of that boy. So I sat him down. I said, "Thomas, don't you never follow me to the coal mine, or ever think of stickin' your head in a coal mine. It's a dog's life!" That's what I told him. "Go to school and get your education, Thomas." And that boy finished school and he never did go in a coal mine.

—NIMROD WORKMAN

THE N & W

WORDS AND MUSIC: NIMROD WORKMAN
(BASED ON JEAN RITCHIE'S "THE L AND N DON'T STOP HERE ANYMORE")

When I raised my fam-i-ly in Chat-ta-roy___ hol-ler The coal train right by___ my___ door. Now it's sit-tin' in the yard all rust-y and emp-ty And the N & W___ train don't stop here no more.

When Thom-as was a ver-y___ small boy___ Set him up___ on my___ knee, "Tom, you go to school and___ learn your num-___bers Don't be an old coal___ mi-ner like___ me."

When I raised my family in Chattaroy holler
The coal train run right by my door.
Now it's sittin' in the yard all rusty and empty
And the N & W train don't stop here no more.

When Thomas was a very small boy
Set him up on my knee,
"Tom, you go to school and learn your numbers
Don't be an old coal miner like me."

My children, they thought I'se a rich man,
Had scrip to buy that company store,
But I go down to old Williamson town with my pocket all empty,
Lord, my hair as white as snow.

The man that made that big machinery
He's taken out all my coal,
He's leavin' children hungry,
And he's robbin' your good land poor.

I don't see what's wrong with that government—
They won't protect my place nor me.
When Rockefeller gets all that big machinery,
He's gonna turn it over to me.
I'm gonna take it to the Atlantic Ocean,
I'm gonna dump it in the middle of the sea.

Costa Manos, Magnum Photos

DREADFUL MEMORIES

WORDS: SARAH OGAN GUNNING
MUSIC: "PRECIOUS MEMORIES"

Dread—ful mem'ries, how they lin-ger, How they ev-er flood my soul,

How the work-ers and their child-ren Died from

hun-ger and from cold.

Dreadful memories, how they linger,
How they ever flood my soul,
How the workers and their children
Died from hunger and from cold.

Hungry fathers, wearied mothers
Living in those dreadful shacks,
Little children cold and hungry
With no clothing on their backs.

Dreadful gun-thugs and stool-pigeons
Always flock around our door.
What's the crime that we've committed?
Nothing, only that we're poor.

Oh, those memories, how they haunt me
Makes me want to organize
Makes me want to help the workers
Make them open up their eyes.

When I think of all the heartaches
And all the things that we've been through,
Then I wonder how much longer
And what a working man can do.

Really, friends, it doesn't matter
Whether you are black or white.
The only way you'll ever change things
Is to fight and fight and fight.

We will have to join the union,
They will help you find a way
How to get a better living
And for your work get better pay.

I was a coal miner's daughter and a coal miner's wife. And I lived in southeastern Kentucky the biggest part of my life.

In the early thirties I had one of my babies starve to death. It literally happened—people starved to death. Not only my own baby, but the neighbors' babies. You seed them starve to death too. And all you could do was go over and help wash and dress 'em and lay 'em out and sit with the mothers until they could put 'em away.

In some of the mines you had to work for so long, and load so many tons of coal before you was allowed to even rent one of them old company houses. And they was just what you'd call a shack now. They had one bedroom, and a front room ('course you used 'em all for bedrooms—you had to), and a kitchen. There was no water in the house. You got the water from a pump or someplace else.

Even when you worked at the best coal mines, what little money you made, they paid you in scrip, and you had to spend it at the company store. And everything cost at least three times as much as it would if you could go downtown to shop. But you wasn't allowed to do that. If you did, they'd fire you from the job. They'd go in the coal mines and work for maybe $2 a day and the biggest part of it went for powder to shoot the coal—they had to shoot their own coal—and they had to buy carbide for a light, and they had to buy the lamps that they put the carbide in. By the time they got through that, well you was lucky if you could draw $1 in scrip. Well you can imagine how much you could get for it in the company store. That was the best mines . . . and the best times.

That, and other things in my life, is what I composed the songs about. These hardships I went through in the Kentucky mountains—and not just me, but a lot of other people too.

I think I'm as good as anybody in the world. I don't have as much education as a lot of people because I was poor and I never had a chance to get it. I took what little I was given and made something of it.

I never was ashamed of myself or my parents in my life. I know I was poor, and I've been hungry many of a time. And I done the very best I could with what little I had to do with. I'm not ashamed of being a hillbilly—I'm proud of it. Some of them hard knocks I had has kept me alive many of a time—because I did have 'em and I learned from 'em.

—SARAH OGAN GUNNING

Jim Marshall

COME ALL YOU COAL MINERS

WORDS AND MUSIC: SARAH OGAN GUNNING

Come all you coal min-ers wher – ev – er you may be And lis-ten to a sto-ry that I'll re-late to thee. My name is noth-ing ex-tra, but the truth to you I'll tell; I am a coal min-er's wife, I'm sure I wish you well.

Come all you coal miners wherever you may be
And listen to a story that I'll relate to thee.
My name is nothing extra, but the truth to you I'll tell;
I am a coal miner's wife, I'm sure I wish you well.

I was born in old Kentucky, in a coal camp born and bred,
I know all about the pinto beans, bulldog gravy & cornbread,
And I know how the coal miners work and slave in the coal mines
    every day,
For a dollar in the company store, for that is all they pay.

Coal mining is the most dangerous work in our land today
With plenty of dirty slaving work, and very little pay.
Coal miner won't you wake up, and open your eyes and see
What the dirty capitalist system is doing to you and me.

They take your very life blood, they take our children's lives,
They take fathers away from children, and husbands away from wives.
Oh, miner, won't you organize wherever you may be?
And make this a land of freedom for workers like you and me.

Dear miner, they will slave you 'til you can't work no more,
And what'll you get for your living but a dollar in a company store,
A tumble-down shack to live in, snow and rain pours in the top.
You have to pay the company rent, your paying never stops.

I am a coal miner's wife, I'm sure I wish you well
Let's sink this capitalist system in the darkest pits of hell.

We had a mighty rough time to get the United Mine Workers started. The thugs killed people and tied 'em to the backs of trucks; they hauled 'em down Tug River.

The union put women and children in tents. And the thugs come along, catch the men gone, they'd go in the tents —children laying on quilts on the floor, cryin' hungry . . . nothing to eat but milk—these thugs would take kerosene and pour it in their milk.

—NIMROD WORKMAN

Ludlow, Colorado, 1914

WHICH SIDE ARE YOU ON?

WORDS: FLORENCE REECE
MUSIC: "LAY THE LILY LOW"

Come all of you good work-ers, Good news to you I'll tell___ Of how the good old un-ion Has come in here to dwell. Which side are you on? Which side are you on?

© 1947 by Stormking Music, Inc.

Come all of you good workers,
Good news to you I'll tell
Of how the good old union
Has come in here to dwell.
      Which side are you on?
      Which side are you on?
      Which side are you on?
      Which side are you on?

My daddy was a miner
And I'm a miner's son,
And I'll stick with the union
Till ev'ry battle's won.
      Which side are you on? etc.

They say in Harlan County
There are no neutrals there;
You'll either be a union man
Or a thug for J. H. Blair.
      Which side are you on? etc.

Oh, workers, can you stand it?
Oh, tell me how you can.
Will you be a lousy scab
Or will you be a man?
      Which side are you on? etc.

Don't scab for the bosses,
Don't listen to their lies.
Us poor folks haven't got a chance
Unless we organize.
      Which side are you on? etc.

Sheriff J. H. Blair and his men came to our house in search of Sam—that's my husband—he was one of the union leaders. I was home alone with our seven children. They ransacked the whole house and then kept watch outside, waiting to shoot Sam down when he came back. But he didn't come home that night.

Afterward I tore a sheet from a calendar on the wall and wrote the words to "Which Side Are You On?" to an old Baptist hymn, "Lay the Lily Low."

My songs always goes to the underdog—to the worker. I'm one of them and I feel like I've got to be with them. There's no such thing as neutral. You *have* to be on one side or the other. Some people say, "I don't take sides—I'm neutral." There's no such thing. In your own mind you're on one side or the other. In Harlan County there wasn't no neutral. If you wasn't a gun thug, you was a union man. You *had* to be.

—FLORENCE REECE

Harry Simms was a young organizer who came into Kentucky when the miners were on strike. He was murdered on Brush Creek in 1932. He was a real good organizer—he was having a lot of influence, mainly among the young people.

A lot of people had been going up to New York to speak about the miners' plight. Aunt Molly Jackson had gone and was speaking and singing around at mass meetings. And these people didn't believe what was going on in Kentucky. A committee (the Dreiser Committee) came to investigate. They said, "We'll just go and see for ourselves what's going on there." They brought a truckload of food, milk, and clothes for the children.

We was going to form a demonstration to go and meet these people to welcome them to Kentucky. We had organizers to go into different sections—Straight Creek, parts of Harlan County. I was to lead them out of Clear Fork. There was a junction there where they could all come together. Harry Simms and Green Lawson was delegated to go and lead the miners out of Brush Creek.

There was two of these company gun men came along on one of these little cars that travel on the railroad tracks. When they saw Harry Simms and Green Lawson walking up the tracks, they stopped and got off and shot Harry Simms. They weren't interested in killing Green Lawson—they knew he was just a local boy. But Harry Simms was an outsider—as they're so fond of calling them.

I was on the committee to go and claim his body from the chief of police.

—TILLMAN CADLE

THE MURDER OF HARRY SIMMS

WORDS AND MUSIC: JIM GARLAND

Come and lis-ten to my sto-ry, come and lis-ten to my song, I'll tell you of a he-ro who now is dead and gone, I'll tell you of a young lad, his age was just nine-teen, He was the brav-est un-ion man that I have ev-er seen.

Come and listen to my story, come and listen to my song,
I'll tell you of a hero who now is dead and gone,
I'll tell you of a young lad, his age was just nineteen,
He was the bravest union man that I have ever seen.

Harry Simms was a pal of mine, we labored side by side,
Expecting to be shot on sight or taken for a ride
By the dirty coal-operator gun thugs that roamed from town to town
Shooting down the union men where'er they could be found.

Harry Simms and I were parted at 12 o'clock that day
Be careful, my dear comrade, to Harry I did say.
But I must do my duty, was his reply to me,
If I get killed by gun thugs, don't grieve after me.

Harry Simms was walking down the track that bright sunshiny day.
He was a youth of courage, his step was light and gay.
He did not know the gun thugs were hiding on the way
To kill our dear young comrade that bright sunshiny day.

Harry Simms was killed on Brush Creek in 1932,
He organized the miners into the NMU,
He gave his life in struggle, it was all that he could do,
He died for the union, he died for me and you.

It is difficult to describe the atmosphere of war time, the tenseness which prevails over the steep green hills of Harlan County. . . .

The company thugs are equipped with army rifles and with the latest model Savage rifle. They also carry revolvers or automatic pistols, bombs, and bring with them in their cars all the machine guns both heavy and light, that they can handle. Their tactics when raiding mining towns (an almost nightly occurrence) is to set up on the hills heavy machine guns commanding the whole town, so that if a fight starts they can simply wipe it out, men, women and children. They charge into the town with their rifles and light machine guns, and search house after house. They smash all weapons found in the houses, look for literature, union cards, etc. On occasion they blow up the miner's car or his house.

—JACK HILL,
in *The Labor Defender*, 1932

One of the strange things about a situation like that is not just the terror, but that people manage to keep some sense of humanity. I remember being up in Harlan County around that period, people scared to death all the time, and yet they decided to have a square dance.

There was no public place to have a square dance, so everybody would go in and take the furniture out of somebody's front room, take down the stove, let it cool off, move the stove, move the furniture, move everything out, and have a square dance. Dance until about two or three o'clock in the morning, then put up the stove again, bring the furniture back in, and the next day shoot it out with the gun thugs.

—MYLES HORTON

THE L & N DON'T STOP HERE ANYMORE

WORDS AND MUSIC: JEAN RITCHIE

O when I was a curly-headed baby,
My daddy set me down upon his knee;
Said, "Son, you go to school and learn your letters,
Don't be no dusty miner like me."
  For I was born and raised at the mouth of the Hazard Holler,
  Coal cars roarin' and a-rumblin' past my door;
  Now they're standin' rusty, rollin' empty,
  And the L and N don't stop here anymore.

I used to think my daddy was a black man
With scrip enough to buy the company store,
But now he goes downtown with empty pockets
And his face as white as February snow.
  For I was born, etc.

Last night I dreamt I went down to the office
To get my payday like I done before;
Them old cudsy-vines had covered up the doorway
And there was trees and grass, well a-growin' right through the floor.
  For I was born, etc.

I never thought I'd live to love the coal dust;
Never thought I'd pray to hear the tipple roar,
But, Lord, how I wish that grass could change to money,
Them greenbacks fill my pockets once more.
  For I was born, etc.

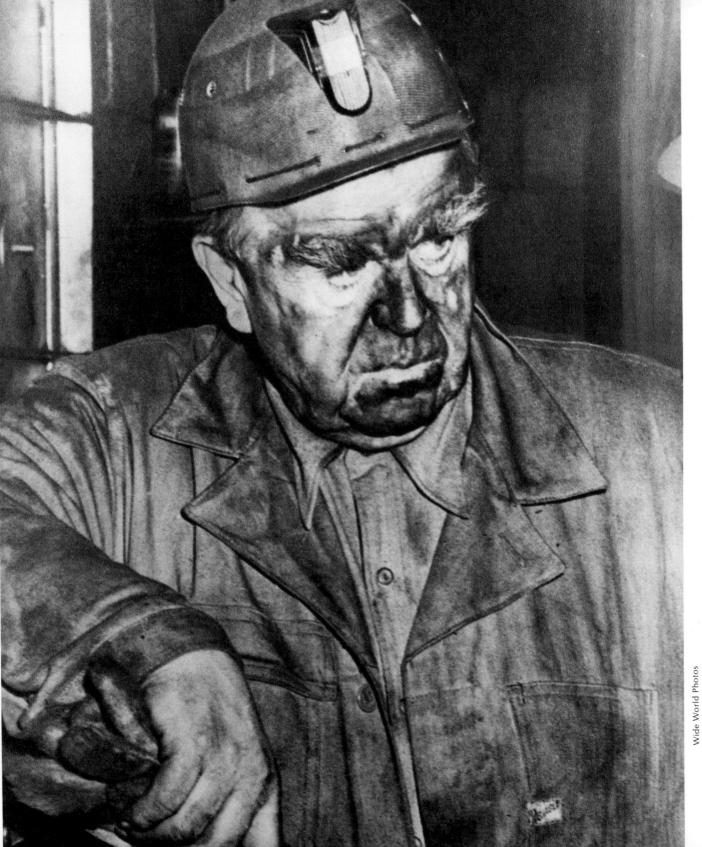

V. MEN WHO DUG EACH OTHER'S GRAVES

Disasters and Negligence in the Coal Industry

If we must grind up human flesh and bones in an industrial machine—in the industrial machine that we call modern America—then, before God, I assert that those who consume coal, and you and I who benefit from that service—because we live in comfort—owe protection to those men first, and we owe security to their families after, if they die. I say it! I voice it! I proclaim it! And I care not who in heaven or hell opposes it!

—JOHN L. LEWIS, 1947

It is hard to tell which is more gripping—the penny-pinching, corner-cutting and profiteering waste of human life in mines still operated today with bland abandon of what the U.S. Bureau of Mines calls "ordinary regard for safety," or the callous result, the history of human carnage in the mines.

The record to date, even the most contemporary chapters of it, is appalling. In the 100 years that partial records of fatal mine accidents have been kept (the early figures are incomplete) more than 120,000 men have died violently in coal mines, an average of 100 every month for a century. The total does not include those who died of what passes for "natural causes" in work that is as notoriously hazardous to health as it is to life and limb. Today, among men aged 60 to 64, the "natural" death rate of miners is eight times that of workers in any other industrial occupation.

—BEN A. FRANKLIN

Earl Dotter

You didn't know when you went in every morning whether you're gonna see daylight outside again. . . . You're under a rock at all times in there; you're under the mountain; you're under there workin' in the bowels of the earth with a mountain up over you. You don't know when a rock's gonna fall that you don't know nothin' about. . . . No, you can't think too much about that because if you did you couldn't get nothin' done. You wouldn't make a dime. You'd be all the time a-dodgin' danger and not workin' and makin' nothin'.

—JIM HAMILTON

Earl Dotter

WEST VIRGINIA MINE DISASTER

WORDS AND MUSIC: JEAN RITCHIE

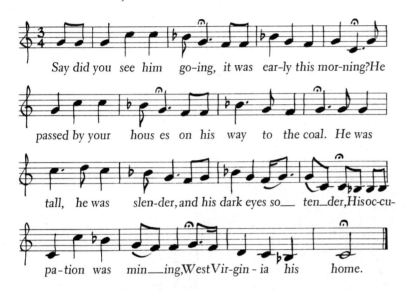

Say did you see him go-ing, it was ear-ly this mor-ning? He
passed by your hous es on his way to the coal. He was
tall, he was slen-der, and his dark eyes so___ ten___der, His oc-cu-
pa-tion was min___ing, West Vir-gin - ia his home.

Say did you see him going, it was early this morning?
He passed by your houses on his way to the coal.
He was tall, he was slender, and his dark eyes so tender,
His occupation was mining, West Virginia his home.

It was just before twelve, I was feeding the children.
Ben Mosely came running to bring us the news;
Number eight is all flooded, many men are in danger,
And we don't know their number, but we fear they're all doomed.

So I picked up the baby and I left all the others
To comfort each other and pray for our own;
There's Timmy fourteen and there's John not much younger,
Their own time soon will be coming to go down the black hole.

O if I had the money to do more than just feed them,
I'd give them good learning, the best could be found.
Then when they'd grow up, they'd be checkers and weighers,
And not spend their time drilling in the dark underground.

Now what can I say to his poor little children?
Or what can I tell his old mother at home?
Or what can I say to my heart that's clear-broken,
To my heart that's clear-broken if my darling is gone?

Say, did you see him going, it was early this morning?
He passed by your houses on his way to the coal.
He was tall, he was slender, and his dark eyes so tender,
His occupation was mining, West Virginia his home.

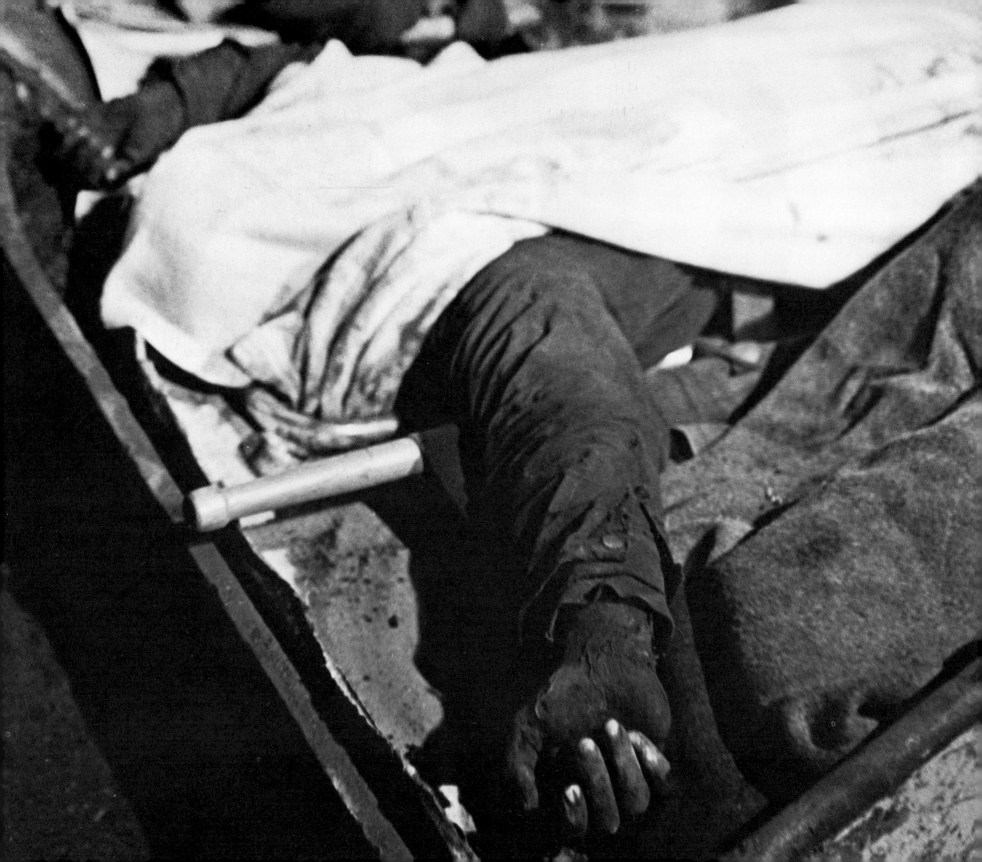

I have seen things happen that caused me to just want to quit. And if there had been anything else that I could have done, I would have quit. I've seen men a-goin' in in the mornin' and maybe just gettin' in their workin' place and the roof come in on 'em. I've knowed men not bein' in their place five minutes 'til they was crushed under a slug of rock 20 feet long, maybe 2 or 3 feet thick. Had to work for ever so long to get 'em out. . . . You get to studyin' at what else you could work at to make a living to stay out of a place like that. It's so unexpected for a man to work and sweat to get to his workin' place and then get killed that way. It's a hard thing to think about a man dyin' in that shape, crushed up so bad that you couldn't even tell who they were.

—JIM HAMILTON

It was cold, snowy, and dark that November 20th, 1968 morning and as I turned the morning news on, the words that were to begin a terrible nightmare hit me. The rumor that there had been an explosion in a Marion County coal mine had just been confirmed; it was the Consolidation Coal Company No. 9 mine at Farmington, West Virginia. All but 21 of the midnight shift were trapped. This was where my husband worked and where the nightmare began.

I was only one of the families involved here, but, as if by magnets, we were drawn to the mine to await their rescue. For ten days waiting, hoping and praying that our men could be saved, but only in vain, for on that tenth day the news was announced to us that "the mine would be sealed because the company officials felt that no human life could live after this time." And so it was to be, 78 good, brave men were sealed in that mine. . . .

This was the second explosion to occur in this same mine within fourteen years, killing 16 men the first time. Yet our husbands' great union leader, Mr. Tony Boyle, stood in front of nationwide television with No. 9 still exploding in the background and announced: "This is one of the safest mines around." Well it kind of makes me shiver all over to think that this was one of the safest. God help the coal miners who work in the other mines.

—MRS. JUDITH ANN HENDERSON,
widow of Paul Frank Henderson

MANNINGTON MINE DISASTER*

WORDS AND MUSIC: HAZEL DICKENS

VERSE - MODERATE TEMPO

We read in the pa-per and the ra-di-o tells____ Us to
raise our chil dren to be mi ners as well.____ Oh, tell them how
safe the mines are to-day____ And to be like your dad-dy, bring
home a big pay.____ Now don't____you be-lieve them, my
boy,____That sto-ry's a lie.____ Re-____
mem-ber the dis-as-ter at the Mann-ing-ton mine____Where
sev-en-ty-eight mi-ners were buried a-live?____Be-cause of
un-safe con-di-tions____your dad-____dy died.____

BRIDGE: INSERT BETWEEN 3RD VERSE AND LAST CHORUS - VERY SLOW TEMPO

There is____ a grave way down in the Mann-ing-ton
mine,____ There is a grave____ way____ down in the
Mann-ing-ton mine.____ Oh,____
what were____ their last____thoughts, what were their cries____
As the flames o-ver-took them____in the Mann-ing-ton
mine.____ Now

(REPEAT FIRST CHORUS)

TAG TO BE SUNG AT THE END OF SONG AFTER LAST CHORUS - MODERATE TEMPO

How can God____ for-give____you, you do know what you've
done____ You've killed my hus-band, now
you____want my____ son.____

* Mannington and Farmington refer to the same mine, which had portals
on two communities; the ridge containing coal separates the two.

© 1971 by Wynwood Music, Inc.

136

We read in the paper and the radio tells
Us to raise our children to be miners as well.
Oh, tell them how safe the mines are today
And to be like your daddy, bring home a big pay.
    Now don't you believe them, my boy,
    That story's a lie.
    Remember the disaster at the Mannington mine
    Where seventy-eight miners were buried alive?
    Because of unsafe conditions your daddy died.

They lure us with money, it sure is a sight
When you may never live to see the daylight,
With your name among the big headlines,
Like that awful disaster at the Mannington mine.
    So don't you believe them, my boy,
    That story's a lie.
    Remember the disaster at the Mannington mine
    Where seventy-eight miners were buried alive?
    Because of unsafe conditions your daddy died.

There's a man in a big house way up on the hill,
Far, far from the shacks where the poor miners live.
He's got plenty of money, Lord everything's fine,
And he has forgotten the Mannington mine,
Yes, he has forgotten the Mannington mine.

There is a grave way down in the Mannington mine,
There is a grave way down in the Mannington mine.
Oh, what were their last thoughts, what were their cries
As the flames overtook them in the Mannington mine.
    So don't you believe them, my boy,
    That story's a lie.
    Remember the disaster at the Mannington mine
    Where seventy-eight good men so uselessly died?
    Oh, don't follow your daddy to the Mannington mine.

How can God forgive you, you do know what you've done
You've killed my husband, now you want my son.

Consolidation Number 9 was in one of the nation's gassiest seams of coal. Eight million cubic feet of methane seeped into Number 9's atmosphere every 24 hours. . . .

. . . In gassy mines such as Number 9, there is no more basic safety procedure than thorough rock dusting. Yet in all 16 inspections made in five years leading up to November 20, 1968, the Bureau of Mines had cited Consol No. 9 for insufficient rock dusting.

—A. BRITTON HUME

On the morning of December 30, 1970, thirty-nine men went underground to work in Finley Coal Company's mines #15 and 16 on Hurricane Creek in Leslie County, Kentucky. Toward noon, one of the men came out to fetch some supplies. That simple errand saved his life. Just as he was heading underground again, the earth around him suddenly shook, and a great rush of smoke and heat and dust came hurtling out of the mine entry, lifting him into the air and leaving him stunned on the ground fifty feet away.

Inside, thirty-eight miners were dead.

—THOMAS N. BETHELL

River Queen Mine, Kentucky

Earl Dotter

THE HYDEN DISASTER

WORDS: SHELVA THOMPSON
MUSIC: "PHILADELPHIA LAWYER"

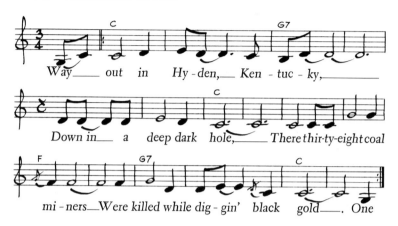

Way__ out in Hy-den,__ Ken-tuc-ky,_____
Down in__ a deep dark hole,__There thir-ty-eight coal
mi-ners__Were killed while dig-gin' black gold__. One

Way out in Hyden, Kentucky,
Down in a deep dark hole,
There 38 coal miners
Were killed while diggin' black gold.

One cold and gloomy morning
On the 30th of December, it's said,
There 38 miners were working—
By one o'clock they were dead.

Thirty-eight men were underground
Eating the noon meal, they say.
But they didn't know that morning
They were digging their very own graves.

Then suddenly it happened,
Down in the Finley death trap,
Thirty-eight miners were murdered,
For safety regulations were slack.

There were 20 or more violations
Down in the Finley coal mine,
But the Feds did nothing about them
For Finley and politics entwine.

The Bureau of Mines held a hearing
To find where the blame did lie.
They didn't blame safety violations,
They blamed two men who had died.

Now Bently and Hibbard were scapegoats
For the coal operators that day.
For the Bureau of Mines blamed two victims
While Finley, though guilty, walked away.

Now Finley is still doing business—
I hear he's doing quite well.
How many more men will be murdered
Before Finley burns in hell?

I worked in the Finley coal mine until the explosion happened. I was standing at the drift mouth and it blowed me about 40 or 50 feet. I was awhile recoverin'. The dust and smoke took my breath. Finally I got my breath and I run between two openings to where the smoke was coming out. I backed up against a bank where the coal had been faced up—for protection. I was tore up and shook up. Then people began gatherin' in. Finally my daughter came and my brother and they got me an ambulance and got me up on the road.

—A. T. COLLINS,
lone survivor of the Hyden disaster

Late in February, the Bureau of Mines sent Charles Finley a letter advising him of proposed fines against his company, based on the violations for which he had been cited. (Investigators discovered that the explosion had been touched off by illegal blasting equipment.) The total came to $53,600 which worked out to $1,410 for each of the thirty-eight men who had died in his mine. To some that might have seemed a bargain. But on March 31 the Finley Company sent a long protest to the Bureau, declining to pay *any* of the fines. The Federal Coal Mine Health and Safety Act of 1969, said the company, "is unconstitutional and void and violates the Constitution of the United States of America," and the attempt to assess a cumulative fine for past violations was, in the opinion of Charles Finley, "cruel and unusual punishment."

—THOMAS N. BETHELL

Phil Primack

The mines has got a lot of laws and rules. If they was carried out there woudn't be as many people getting hurt and getting destroyed. But the thing is they don't carry 'em out. They wink at somebody and get by with too much. A man's life is not worth too much. A man get killed, they'll holler, "It's just another one of them things." They don't care. If you try to get justice, they'll kick you out. They'll starve you out —or anything they can do to you. You have to have pretty good nerve to even live in this country, let alone work in it.

I've held up pretty good so far. I've never had to beg from none of 'em or run from none of 'em. I don't feel like I'll be caught back in the mines myself anymore. I think I'll hunt somethin' else. Been lucky to get by like I have. A man's luck'll finally run out. It don't hang on forever.

—A. T. COLLINS

One hundred thirty million gallons of water swept through the narrow, crowded valley of Buffalo Creek shortly after 8:00 A.M. on Saturday, February 26, 1972. The worst flood in West Virginia history, this man-made disaster left 124 people dead, 7 people missing, 4,000 homeless, fourteen communities destroyed.

Survivors' accounts, journalists' unanswered questions, and the disappearance of the mining company official most directly involved—together with the remembrance of past disasters—brought a stunned citizenry to its feet. The public was jolted from the depths of sorrow and anguish to a sense of outrage and anger that continues to burn.

For the Buffalo Creek disaster, like the recent coal mine tragedies at Farmington, West Virginia, and Hyden, Kentucky, could have been prevented—it need not have happened. Clearly and simply, people living downstream from the Buffalo Mining Company's coal refuse dam at Saunders were the victims of gross negligence.

—from *Disaster on Buffalo Creek:*
A Citizens' Report on Criminal Negligence
in a West Virginia Mining Community

BUFFALO CREEK

WORDS: DOUG AND RUTH YARROW
MUSIC: "1913 MASSACRE, CALUMET, MICHIGAN"

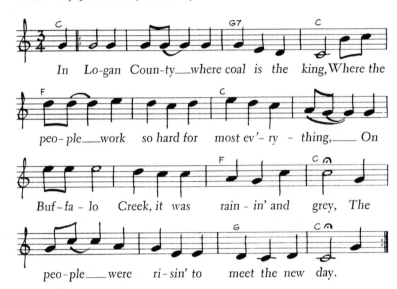

In Lo-gan Coun-ty___where coal is the king, Where the peo-ple___work so hard for most ev'-ry - thing,___ On Buf-fa - lo Creek, it was rain - in' and grey, The peo-ple___were ri - sin' to meet the new day.

In Logan County where coal is the king,
Where the people work so hard for most everything,
On Buffalo Creek, it was rainin' and grey,
The people were risin' to meet the new day.

The bacon was a-sizzlin' and the coffee was poured,
But the dam up the hollow wouldn't hold any more.
Water raged down that valley, smashed town after town,
Homes dashed to pieces, whole families was drowned.

And how could it happen? said, how could it be?
That dam it belonged to the coal company.
An act of God, the bosses did cry.
But God ain't that cruel, we can see through your lie.

Who ordered the dozers to build up that dam?
And who's livin' high on the work of our hands?
Who takes our coal but don't share in the fear?
Whose greed for money has cost us so dear?

When coal comes out of the earth, there is refuse—rock and other unburnable material. It is sorted out before the coal is loaded into railroad cars, and trucked away to be dumped wherever convenient. The dump—called a "gob pile" or "slag heap"—grows steadily. Over a period of time it may stretch hundreds of yards across an entire valley, growing hundreds of feet high as the dumping continues.

—THOMAS N. BETHELL

We believe it was an act of God. There was nothing wrong with the gob pile, except that it was incapable of holding the water God poured into it.

—Pittston spokesman in New York

The dam was not properly planned from an engineering view . . . and failed. . . .

—U.S. GEOLOGICAL SURVEY,
preliminary disaster report

Some people saw it coming—"a solid wall of waste and water, must have been 50 feet high," as one man described the sight later. Mud and rock and water, the mass moved down Buffalo Creek and took everything with it. Roads disappeared underneath or were torn up and flung ahead. The steel rails of the C&O railroad were lifted and twisted like wet spaghetti; the houses were torn from their foundations and smashed against each other until there was nothing left but old lumber. Bridges were wrenched from their moorings intact and hurled hundreds of yards at a time. Pictures of Jack Kennedy and Jesus Christ rode down through the valley and disappeared under the brown sea. Along with nobody knows how many people. Bodies were found later as far as 25 miles downstream, floating toward the Ohio River.

—THOMAS N. BETHELL

ACT OF MAN

WORDS AND MUSIC: ETHEL BREWSTER, SHELVA THOMPSON, SHELBY STEELE

© 1975 by Ethel Brewster, Shelva Thompson, and Shelby Steele

Down in the valley, where the poor people live,
There came a disaster I'll never forget.
It came one morning around about eight,
They gave them a warning, but it came too late.

The waters came rushing like a big tidal wave.
They ran for the mountains, they ran for the caves.
But the water overtook them, their homes and their lives,
Killing little children, husbands and wives.

Now the coal company squabbled over who was to blame.
They blame it on God, and there damn his name.
For the people who lived there know who was at fault,
For on that sad morning murder was wrought.

Now standing on a hillside, left all alone
A father stood weeping while the coal rolls on.
For the company has no feeling for what they have done—
They killed his wife, his daughter and son.

Now they won't be punished for what they have done—
Just poor people died there, not a rich man or his son.
For they live in fine mansions from the wealth they have stole,
But God will have vengeance, or so I am told.
But God will have vengeance, or so I am told.

THE HATE

WORDS AND MUSIC: JACK WRIGHT

The flood-ing ain't o-ver and the kil-ling ain't done A cas-ket will be car-ried by fa-ther and by son. And a moun-tain-eer hates___ as long as he lives, And the sun___will ne-ver shine___ on the day he for-gives. there's ma-chin-ery in his moun-tains, There's for-eign-ers dig-ging his coal, And it's lea-vin' his peo-___ple hun-gry, Lord, It's lea-vin' his poor land broke.

The flooding ain't over and the killing ain't done—
A casket will be carried by father and by son.
And a mountaineer hates as long as he lives,
And the sun will never shine on the day he forgives.
　'Cause there's machinery in his mountains,
　There's foreigners digging his coal,
　And it's leavin' his people hungry, Lord,
　It's leavin' his poor land broke.

His burden is heavy and his nights have grown cold.
He's strong as an oak but too soon he's grown old.
But for food for his children and for the love of his wife,
He'll stand like a giant and he'll give his life.
　'Cause there's machinery, etc.

In the wake of the Buffalo Creek Disaster, the Pittston Company is sitting pretty,* counting its money, still refusing to accept responsibility for the deaths of at least 124 people, and not worrying very much about being called to account.

The Interior Department has quietly ignored three departmental investigative reports that leave no doubt at all about where the responsibility lies for the Buffalo Creek disaster. Pittston, these reports show, built an unsafe dam, had ample reason to know it was unsafe, continued to use it anyway, continued in fact to pump sludge-filled water into the lake behind the dam through the night of February 25 even though company officials were already afraid the dam might let go.

Interior's own investigative reports leave no doubt that the worst flood in West Virginia history could have been prevented. They suggest that a safe dam could have been built for as little as $50,000. They show clearly that the dam was built in violation of three different West Virginia laws, and in violation of federal regulations adopted as part of the 1969 Coal Mine Health and Safety Act.†

—THOMAS N. BETHELL

* The Pittston Company produced earnings in 1972 of $24,097,000, or $1.43 per share. Historic highs were reached in revenues, working capital, total assets, shareholders' equity, and book value per share.
—from *Report to the Shareholders of Pittston*

† In July, 1974, the Pittston Company agreed to a $13.5 million damage settlement for 625 survivors who sued the company for damages. The out-of-court agreement was, in effect, the first public admission that Pittston was guilty of massive negligence.

Earl Dotter

Asking a coal miner to work under unsupported roof is like sentencing him to the death penalty.

This nation expresses continual outrage when a major coal mine disaster occurs. But when miners die in ones and twos under unsupported roof there are few headlines and precious little outrage. But to us coal miners those who die are not names on the inside pages of a newspaper; they are our fathers, brothers, and sons. We are tired of mourning coal mine fatalities. We intend to prevent them.

The nation's highest court has banned the death penalty from the halls of justice. The United Mine Workers is banning it from the nation's coal mines. Coal will be mined under proper conditions or coal won't be mined at all.

—MIKE TRBOVICH,
Vice-President, UMWA

There is a basic question raised anew by each coal industry disaster: Whether the people of Appalachia can any longer afford this senseless destruction of their lives, their land, and their democratic institutions; or whether the ownership and operation of the coal mines should be brought under democratic control to benefit all the people. All too clearly the mask has been torn away, revealing the ugly truth that powerful coal interests dominate the government, the environment, and the Appalachian way of life to the detriment of all its citizens. Discussion and action are needed now to transform King Coal, the tyrant, into Citizen Coal, the servant of all—before and not after another coal disaster.

—*from Disaster at Buffalo Creek*

*Jack Smith, one of the leaders of
the Disabled Miners and Widows
Strike in West Virginia in 1970*

THERE IS A FOUNTAIN

ORIGINAL WORDS AND MUSIC: WILLIAM COWPER AND LOWELL MASON
NEW WORDS: JOAN BOYD

There__ is a foun-tain filled with blood, The
blood of our moun-tain men so brave, Men who
worked to-geth-er in the black coal pits, Men who
dug each oth-er's graves. Men who dug each oth-er's
graves, oh, God, Men who dug each oth__ er's
graves, Men who worked to-geth-er in the black coal pits, Men who
dug each oth - er's graves.

There is a fountain filled with blood,
The blood of our mountain men so brave,
Men who worked together in the black coal pits,
Men who dug each other's graves.
Men who dug each other's graves, oh, God,
Men who dug each other's graves,
Men who worked together in the black coal pits,
Men who dug each other's graves.

There is a river that runs with tears,
The tears of our children and our wives
For their fathers and husbands, good mining men,
Who so senselessly have died.
Who so senselessly have died, oh, God,
Who so senselessly have died,
For their fathers and husbands, good mining men,
Who so senselessly have died.

There is a river so deep and wide,
It once was so beautiful and grand,
'Til the stripminers tore off our mountainsides,
Now it runs brown with the blood of our land.
Now it runs brown with the blood of our land, oh, God,
It runs brown with the blood of our land,
'Til the stripminers tore off our mountainsides,
Now it runs brown with the blood of our land.

There is a fountain filled with blood,
The blood of our land and of our men,
Let us stand beneath its powerful flood,
Be revived to fight and win.
Be revived to fight and win, oh, God,
Be revived to fight and win,
Let us stand beneath its powerful flood,
Be revived to fight and win.

VI. DON'T YOU WANT TO GO TO THAT LAND?

Protest and Change in the Coal Fields

The miner realizes he's been taken. In the area of black lung, he was destroyed badly. In the area of the destruction of his home, his mountains that he loves so dearly, he's been taken, and he's hitting back.

He used to curse and spit his lungs out on the ground. Just curse. Now his curses are taking direction. He's finding his enemies.

—JOHN TILLER

DON'T YOU WANT TO GO TO THAT LAND?

WORDS: NIMROD WORKMAN
MUSIC: ADAPTATION OF TRADITIONAL SPIRITUAL

Don't you want to go to that land,
Don't you want to go to that land,
Don't you want to go to that land where I go?
Don't you want to go to that land?
I'm a-gonna go to that land.
Don't you want to go to that land where I go?

Be no strip mining in that land where I go.
Be no strip mining in that land where I go.
I'm a-gonna go to that land.
Don't you want to go to that land,
Don't you want to go to that land where I go?

No low wages in that land where I go.
No low wages in that land where I go.
I'm a-gonna go to that land.
Don't you want to go to that land,
Don't you want to go to that land where I go?

No exploitation in that land where I go.
No exploitation in that land where I go.
I'm a-gonna go to that land.
Don't you want to go to that land,
Don't you want to go to that land where I go?

Be no black lung in that land where I go.
Be no black lung in that land where I go.
I'm a-gonna go to that land.
Don't you want to go to that land,
Don't you want to go to that land where I go?

Be no politicians in that land where I go.
Be no politicians in that land where I go.
I'm a-gonna go to that land.
Don't you want to go to that land,
Don't you want to go to that land where I go?

Be no sickness in that land where I go.
Be no sickness in that land where I go.
I'm a-gonna go to that land.
Don't you want to go to that land,
Don't you want to go to that land where I go?

No Tony Boyle in that land where I go.
No Tony Boyle in that land where I go.
I'm a-gonna go to that land.
Don't you want to go to that land,
Don't you want to go to that land where I go?

    Don't you want to go to that land,
    Don't you want to go to that land where I go?
    Don't you want to go to that land?
    I'm a-gonna go to that land.
    Don't you want to go to that land where I go?

Nimrod Workman speaks before
singing in West Virginia.

BLUE DIAMOND MINES

WORDS AND MUSIC: JEAN RITCHIE

I re-mem-ber the ways___ in the by-gone days When we was all in our prime,___ How us and John L.___ we give the old man hell Down in the Blue Dia-mond mines,___ When the whis-tle would blow___ and the roos-ter-crowed Two hours be-fore___ day-light,___ When a man done his best___ and he earned his good rest And had sev-en___teen dol-lars___ at night.___

CHORUS

In the mines, in the mines, In the Blue Dia-mond mines___ I have worked my life___ a-way___ In the

158

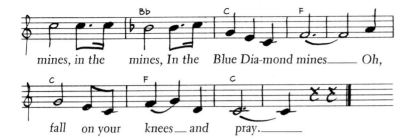

mines, in the mines, In the Blue Dia-mond mines____ Oh,

fall on your knees__ and pray.____

I remember the ways in the bygone days
When we was all in our prime,
How us and John L. we give the old man hell
Down in the Blue Diamond mines,
When the whistle blowed and the rooster crowed
Two hours before daylight,
When a man done his best and he earned his good rest
And had seventeen dollars at night.
    In the mines, in the mines,
    In the Blue Diamond mines
    I've worked my life away
    In the mines, in the mines,
    In the Blue Diamond mines
    Oh, fall on your knees and pray.

You old black gold, you've gotten my lungs
And your dust has darkened my home.
Now that I'm old you're turning your back—
Where else can an old miner go?
When it's Alooma Block and it's Big Leatherwood
And now it's Blue Diamond too.
The pits they are closing, get another job—
What else can an old miner do?
    In the mines, etc.

Your union is dead and they shake their heads,
Say mining has had its day,
But they're strip-mining up on my mountain top
And they pay me three dollars a day.
Now you might get a little poke of welfare meal,
Get a little sack of welfare flour,
But I'll tell you right now that you won't qualify
Till you work for a quarter an hour.
    In the mines, etc.

John L. had a dream but it's broken it seems
And the union is lettin' us down.
Last week they took away my hospital card,
Said why don't you leave this old town?
Now I'll go downtown and hang around
And maybe it ain't so bad,
But they meet you at the door when you go to come in,
Say what did you bring us, Dad?
    In the mines, etc.

THE ROVING PICKETS

In the 1950s and early '60s the coal boom was over. Mines were shutting down. There was no kind of relief program except welfare. There were no jobs. People were starting to go to Detroit and Dayton. People had nothing to do. They were hungry. A lot of them did have their union welfare cards and their hospital they could be taken to if they got sick.

Well, when the union started selling the hospitals and taking their welfare cards away, that was all they had left; and when you take all a man's got, that's when something's going to happen. People were literally starving to death . . . and they were mad. A fat dog won't fight. A hungry dog's the one that fights.

—BUCK MAGGARD

THE BLIND FIDDLER

WORDS AND MUSIC: ERIC ANDERSON
BASED ON SONG BY EMMA DUSENBURY

I lost my eyes in the Har-lan___ pits in the year of 'fifty-___ six While pul-ling___ a fault-y drill-chain that was___ out___ of fix. It bound-ed from the wall and there con-cealed my doom I am a blind___ fid-dl-er, far___ from my___ home.

Council of the Southern Mountains, Inc.

I lost my eyes in the Harlan pits in the year of '56
While pulling a faulty drill-chain that was out of fix.
It bounded from the wall and there concealed my doom—
I am a blind fiddler, far from my home.

I went up into Louisville to visit Dr. Laine.
He operated on one of my eyes and still it's just the same.
The Blue Ridge can't support me, it just ain't got the room.
Would a wealthy mine owner like to hear a fiddler's tune?

With politics and threatenin' words the owners do control.
The unions have all left us a long, long time ago.
Machinery lying scattered, no drill sound in the mine.
For all the good a miner is, he might as well be blind.

I used to work a long fourteen for a short eight bucks a day.
You're lucky to be workin', that's what the owners say.
And if you start complainin', you better aim to keep it low—
They'll soon be cuttin' your food stamps down at the company store.

Cardboard on the window and plastic for the door,
Hungry children lying all on the cabin floor.
They need welders in Chicago, I've heard that tale before—
How many thousand miners have made that trip before?

The lights are burning brightly, there's laughter in the town;
Back home it's dark and empty, not a miner can be found.
They're in some lonesome holler where the sun refuse to shine,
And the baby's screams are muffled by the sweetness of their wine.

With a wife and four young children depending now on me,
However can I help them, my God, I cannot see.
Through the Blue Ridge Mountains I am forced to roam—
I am a blind fiddler far from my home.

Orb Caudill

Phil Primack

When the board of directors of the UMWA's Welfare and Retirement Fund made the decision to revoke the medical cards of all members . . . working for coal companies who had failed to sign the national agreement, it left the coal miners throughout the area without any health and welfare protection whatsoever, . . . which caused a spontaneous uprising of tens of thousands of coal miners in eastern Kentucky.

Because of the roving nature of their work, traveling by automobile from mine to mine through several counties in eastern Kentucky and closing down mines as they went, the news media promptly dubbed them "the roving pickets." Immediately a campaign of terror sprang up, such as dynamiting the homes of the roving pickets, dynamiting the homes and churches of those who rendered aid and assistance to the pickets' cause, the burning of coal tipples, dynamiting power lines, blowing up railroad bridges, and other forms of intimidation.

—EVERETTE THARP

161

COME ON FRIENDS
AND LET'S GO DOWN

WORDS: SARAH OGAN GUNNING
MUSIC: "AS I WENT DOWN IN THE VALLEY TO PRAY"

Come on friends and let's go down, Let's go down, let's go down,

Come on friends and let's go down, Down on the picket line.

As I went down on the picket line, To

keep them scabs out of the mine, Who's a going to

win the strike? Come on and we'll show you the way.

VERSE

Went out one morning be-fore day-light, And I was sure we'd

have a fight, But the cap-it-'list scur-vy had

run a-way But we went back the ver-y next day.

© 1965 by Folk Legacy Records

Come on friends and let's go down,
Let's go down, let's go down,
Come on friends and let's go down,
Down on the picket line.

As I went down on the picket line,
To keep them scabs out of the mine,
Who's a-going to win the strike?
Come on and we'll show you the way.
    Come on friends, etc.

Went out one morning before daylight,
And I was sure we'd have a fight,
But the capitalist scurvy had run away
But we went back the very next day.
    Come on friends, etc.

We all went out on the railroad track
To meet them scabs and turn them back,
We win that strike I'm glad to say.
Come on, and we'll show you the way.
    Come on friends, etc.

* This song was written during the National Miners Union strike on Straight Creek, Bell County, Kentucky, in 1932.

Dear Editor:

I recently read a magazine of yours about the labor unrest in Perry county and surrounding counties. I would like very much to get one of these magazines to send to my son in the service. I don't have any money to send you for it, but would you please send me one anyway?

I am a miner's wife. I have been married 26 years to a coal miner and you can't find a harder worker than a coal miner. We have been treated so unfair by our leaders from the sheriff up to the president. I know what it is to be hungry.

My husband has been out of work for 14 months. He worked at a union mine at Leatherwood. Now the company has terminated the union contract (UMWA) and plans to go back to work with scab workers. It isn't just here that all this is happening. The company will say they have to close as they are going in the hole. Then they will re-open with scab laborers that will work for practically nothing as long as the boss smiles at them and gives them a pat on the back. These men just don't realize the amount of people they are hurting or just don't care.

The operators have the money and the miner doesn't have anything but a bad name. You couldn't find better people anywhere in the whole world. But we have our pride too. We are tired of doing without. The operators have beautiful homes, Cadillacs and Aeroplanes to enjoy, and our homes (camp houses, by the way) look like barns.

We don't want what the operators have. All we want is a decent wage and good insurance that will help our families. Is this too much to ask?

The operators wouldn't go in a mine for fifty dollars a day. I've seen my husband come home from work with his clothes frozen to his body from working in the water. I have sat down at a table where we didn't have anything to eat but wild greens picked from the mountain side. There are three families around me, that each family of seven only had plain white gravy and bread for a week is true. Is this progress or what? I just can't understand it.

I have two sons that go to school and they don't even have decent clothes to wear. No one knows our feelings and I'm quite sure the coal operators don't care as long as they get that almighty dollar. Of all the things that were sent here to the Helping Fund (Editor's Note: This is the "relief" fund administered by the Hazard newspaper. See story, January PL.) not one of these needy families received a thing nor did anyone here in camp. Where did it all go? Somebody got a real good vacation with it I suppose. All the newspapers are against us because of political pressure, but our day is coming.

The government talks of retraining. My husband went into the mines in Alabama at the age of 11 with only the second grade of schooling. How could he retrain now, and him 52? It is silly to even think this will help the older miner. All the state thinks about is building up the tourist trade. How will that help us? It would just put more money in the big shots' pockets—not ours. No one would want to spend money to come here for a vacation to see the desolate mine camps and ravaged hills.

Happy A. B. Chandler lost his election by siding against the laboring class of people; by sending the State Militia and State Police in here to use as strikebreakers in 1959. Wilson Wyatt lost because Governor Combs doing the same thing, only in a more subtle way. How can he hope to get elected to the Senate? How does he think Ed Breathitt will fare by endorsing him?

The truth will out someday. I'm sorry I have rambled on like this. It just seems so unjust, especially to the poor.

Please, sir, could you send me a magazine?

Thank you sincerely,

Mrs. Clara Sullivan
Scuddy, Kentucky
Perry County

—letter to *Progressive Labor News*, January, 1963

CLARA SULLIVAN'S LETTER

WORDS: MALVINA REYNOLDS
MUSIC: PETER SEEGER

Mis-ter Ed-i-tor, if you choose___, Please send me a co-py of the lab-or news;___ I've got a son in the In-fan-try___, And he'd be migh-ty glad___ to see___ That someone, some-where, now and then, Thinks a-bout the lives of the min-ing men,___ In Per-ry Coun-ty.___

Dear Mister Editor, if you choose,
Please send me a copy of the labor news;
I've got a son in the Infantry,
And he'd be mighty glad to see
That someone, somewhere, now and then,
Thinks about the lives of the mining men,
    In Perry County.

In Perry County and thereabout
We miners simply had to go out.
It was long hours, substandard pay,
Then they took our contract away.
Fourteen months is a mighty long time
To face the goons from the picket line
    In Perry County.

I'm twenty-six years a miner's wife,
There's nothing harder than a miner's life,
But there's no better man than a mining man,
Couldn't find better in all this land.
The deal they get is a rotten deal,
Mountain greens and gravy meal,
    In Perry County.

We live in barns that the rain comes in
While operators live high as sin,
Ride Cadillac cars and drink like a fool
While our kids lack clothes to go to school.
Sheriff Combs he has it fine,
He runs the law and owns a mine
    In Perry County.

What operator would go dig coal
For even fifty a day on the mine pay-roll!
Why, after work my man comes in
With his wet clothes frozen to his skin,
Been digging coal so the world can run
And operators can have their fun
    In Perry County.

When folks sent money to the Hazard Press
To help the strikers in distress,
They gave that money, yours and mine,
To the scabs who crossed the picket line,
And the state militia and the F.B.I.
Just look on while miners die
    In Perry County.

I believe the truth will out some day
That we're fighting for jobs at decent pay.
We're just tired of doing without,
And that's what the strike is all about,
And it helps to know that folks like you
Are telling the story straight and true,
    About Perry County.

The women were the strongest ones on the picket lines. The men weren't goin' to do anything. The women just showed the way. You know men's always good about sneakin' around after dark where nobody can't see 'em. The women, they do it openly. I don't think it was just the thing of using their sex for protection either; they were just damned determined. That's all you can say about 'em.

When the women went off the picket lines, that's when the whole thing just fell apart.

Clara Sullivan was just a coal miner's wife until she got hungry and mad, like all the other women did.

—BUCK MAGGARD

The roving pickets was not really organized by anybody. It was a spontaneous kind of thing. I don't know where it started. Probably some guy one morning just got tired of conditions and poured his water out of his water bucket and went back home. And the whole thing . . . just happened.

The first morning I went on the picket line, me and another guy were going out of Montgomery Creek and we looked down the road and we seen all these jeeps coming. It was the National Guard. They pulled up to us, the captain and this black guy with a Tommy gun next to him, and they asked us where we was a-goin'.

We said, "We're goin' to Vicco."

And they said, "Good, get in . . . we're goin' up the road . . . we'll give you a ride." So we just got into the back of the jeep and went on up the road.

We were goin' to the Scratch-Back railroad crossing—that's where the picket line was, that's where we were going to report in for duty that morning.

So we rode down and the captain said, "This is as far as we're goin', this railroad crossing here."

We said, "That's all right, that's as far as we're goin' too."

So we got out and there was this big cliff hanging out over the highway, so we went over and joined the rest of the pickets under that cliff. The National Guard, they just drove on over across the tracks and lined up with their guns and things. And we were sittin' there drinkin' coffee and swappin' lies, and they were over there watching us with machine guns.

That was my first day on the picket line. And that's a hell of an experience to get escorted by the National Guard down to the picket line.

The funniest thing that happened that day, there was a guy up on the mountain squirrel hunting. We heared his dog barkin' and we knowed he had a squirrel up a tree. He barked about ten minutes and this old guy finally got to the tree where he was at, and he shot the squirrel out. And when he done that, you should have seen them damn guardsmen scurryin' around. They thought they'd done been attacked from the mountains. I was just lookin' for 'em to open fire on that poor old guy with that 50-calibre machine gun.

—BUCK MAGGARD

Every time there is a strike on hand, the law is automatically against the miners—the state militia, state police, county sheriffs, all of them. They use every means in the world to prevent them from striking and to prevent them from shutting down mines. The same thing happened to the roving pickets. The state militia had to be called in.

There was lots of dynamiting going on—power companies' facilities were blown up, and a lot of railroad tracks, bridges, and things. Nobody knows specifically who did it, don't know whether it was the operators done it. They've been accused of doing it in order to lay it on the miners.

The strike and the union finally died down and the union went out. There's not a union mine in Perry County at this time.

—EVERETTE THARP

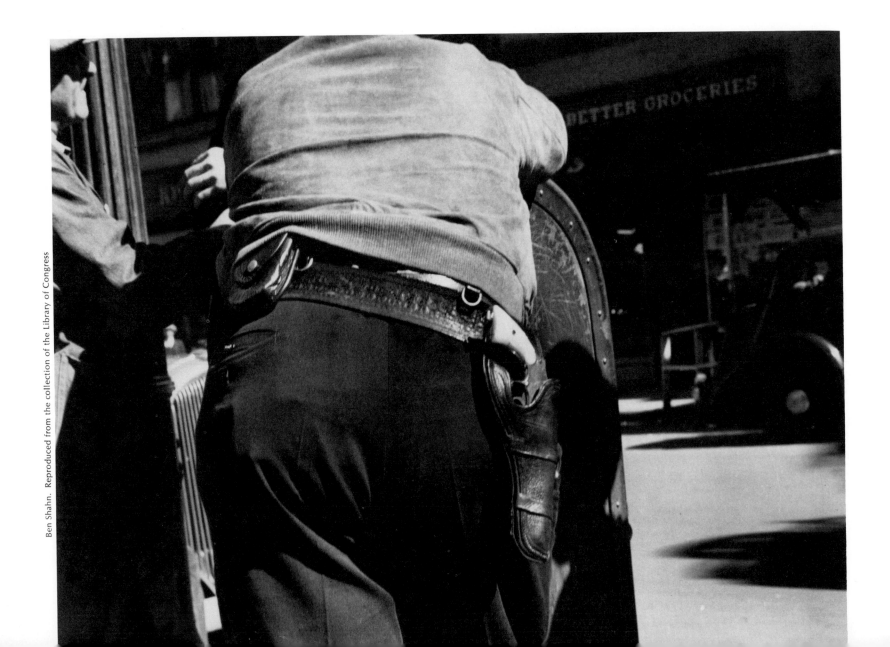

THE HIGH SHERIFF OF HAZARD

WORDS AND MUSIC: TOM PAXTON

Now the high sher-iff of Haz-ard is a hard work-in' man To be a fine sher-iff is his on-ly plan With his hands in our pock-ets he'll take what he can For he's the high sher-iff of Haz-ard. He went through my pock-ets and searched them with care But nar-y a nick-el or pen-ny was there So I got thir-ty days and some bumps in my hair God bless the high sher-iff of Haz-ard.

On duty during strike, Morgan-town, West Virginia, 1935. Farm Security Administration photo

Now the high sheriff of Hazard is a hard workin' man
To be a fine sheriff is his only plan
With his hands in our pockets he'll take what he can
For he's the high sheriff of Hazard.

He went through my pockets and searched them with care
But nary a nickel or penny was there
So I got 30 days and some bumps in my hair
God bless the high sheriff of Hazard.

He caught me one evening and here's what he said
You look like a Russian, you look like a red
And if you are fond of your skin and your head
Beware the high sheriff of Hazard.

I thanked him politely, I thanked him for all
And five minutes later I made a phone call
To call a strike meeting at our union hall
And damn the high sheriff of Hazard.

Now men there are many who sweat out their lives
To scratch out a living for children and wives
They sweat for their pennies while the mine owner thrives
With the blessings of the high sheriff of Hazard.

And when union men strike and the troubles come in
The high sheriff's word is the mine owner's bond
He's a mine owner too, you know which side he's on
He's the wealthy high sheriff of Hazard.

Well it seems to be so since this world first began
That some men are willing to scheme and to plan
To gouge out a fortune from the poor working man
For example the high sheriff of Hazard.

But the answer is simple, the answer is clear
We'll all get together with nothing to fear
And throw the old bastard right out on his ear
Farewell to the high sheriff of Hazard.

The conditions continued to deteriorate and in January, 1964, the Committee for Miners in New York chartered a bus to take a group of unemployed miners to Washington D.C. This campaign was two fold; first to alert the nation as to the economic conditions in Eastern Kentucky; and second, to get Federal relief for all the people of poverty who had been made idle by automation. We visited senators and representatives throughout Appalachia and also various governmental department heads.

We asked for an appointment with President Johnson and received an invitation to meet with his aide, Mr. George Reedy. It was in this discussion that Mr. Reedy suggested that we come back home and organize so as to be in a better position to aid and assist the Government to carry out their War on Poverty Program. This campaign was so successful that before we left Washington, D.C., the first million dollars was appropriated for the unemployed in seven Eastern Kentucky Counties.

—EVERETTE THARP

Robert Cooper

THE BLACK LUNG MOVEMENT

It is estimated that more than 100,000 current and former miners suffer from coal miners' pneumoconiosis, more commonly called *black lung.*

—from the *U.S. Surgeon General's Report* (1967)

BLACK LUNG BLUES

WORDS AND MUSIC: MIKE PAXTON
AS SUNG BY GEORGE TUCKER

I went to the doc-tor, could-n't hard-ly get my breath

Went to the doc-tor, could-n't hard-ly get my breath The

doc-tor said you got some-thing that well could mean your death. With this

pneu-mo-co-ni-o-sis, the black lung___ blues

Pneu-mo-co-ni-o-sis, the black lung___ blues If you got

one, you got the oth-er, an-y way you lose.

I went to the doctor, couldn't hardly get my breath
Went to the doctor, couldn't hardly get my breath
The doctor said you got something that well could mean your death.
　　With this pneumoconiosis, the black lung blues
　　Pneumoconiosis, the black lung blues
　　If you got one, you got the other, any way you lose.

I've always been a miner, breathed coal dust all my life
I've always been a miner, breathed coal dust all my life
Too old to learn a new trade, what can I tell my wife?
　　With this pneumoconiosis, etc.

I'll tell nobody nothin', I'll just keep workin' on
I'll tell nobody nothin', I'll just keep workin' on
The kids need all their schoolin' before I'm dead and gone.
　　With this pneumoconiosis, etc.

When I get to Heaven, St. Peter's going to cry
When I get to Heaven, St. Peter's going to cry
When I tell him the reason this poor boy had to die.
　　With this pneumoconiosis, the black lung blues
　　Pneumoconiosis, the black lung blues
　　I'll lay down my pick and shovel, lose these black lung blues.

BLACK LUNG

WORDS AND MUSIC: HAZEL DICKENS

He's had more hard luck than most men could stand, The mines was his first love, but never his friend, He's lived a hard life, and hard he'll die, Black Lung's done got him, his time is nigh.

He's had more hard luck than most men could stand,
The mines was his first love, but never his friend,
He's lived a hard life, and hard he'll die,
Black Lung's done got him, his time is nigh.

Black Lung, Black Lung, you're just biding your time,
Soon all this suffering I'll leave behind,
But I can't help but wonder what God had in mind,
To send such a devil to claim this soul of mine.

He went to the boss man, but he closed the door,
Well, it seems you're not wanted when you're sick and you're poor,
You're not even covered in their medical plans,
And your life depends on the favors of man.

Down in the poor house on starvation's plan,
Where pride is a stranger and doomed is a man,
His soul full of coal dust 'til his body's decayed,
And everyone but Black Lung has done turned him away.

Black Lung, Black Lung, oh your hand's icy cold,
As you reach for my life and you torture my soul,
Coal dust and water hole down in that dark cave,
Where I spent my life's blood, digging my own grave.

Down at the grave yard the boss man came,
With his little bunch of flowers, dear God, what a shame,
Take back those flowers, don't you sing no sad songs,
The die has been cast, now a good man is gone.

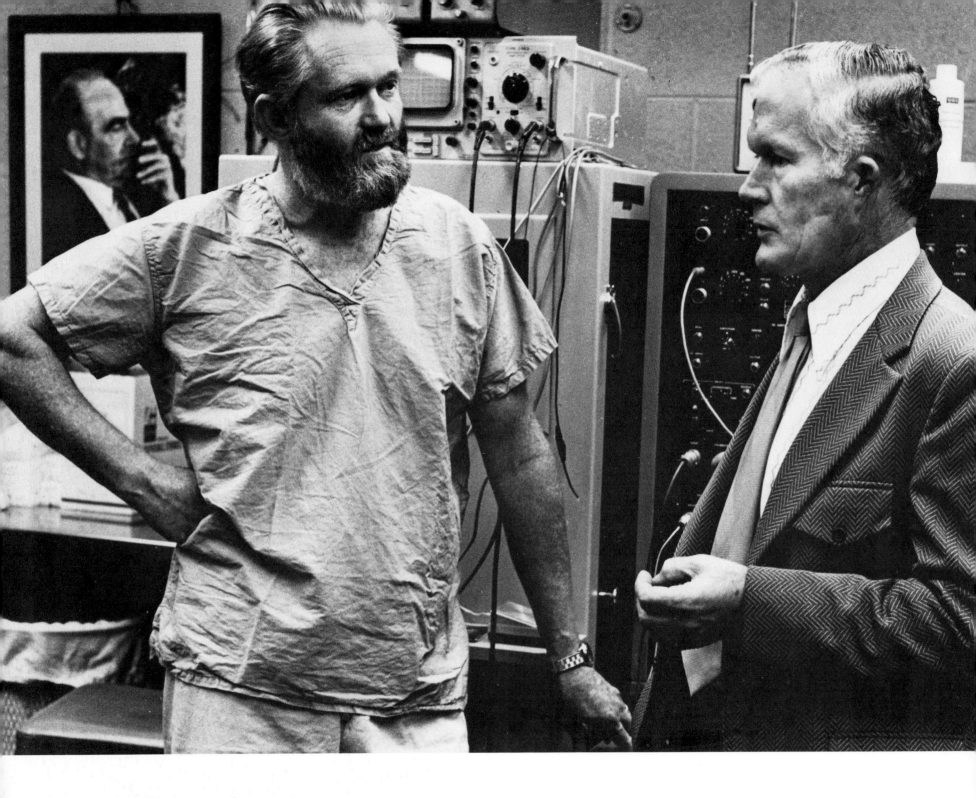

*Dr. Donald Rasmussen and
Arnold Miller*

At work you are covered with dust. It's in your hair, your clothes, and your skin. The rims of your eyes are coated with it. It gets between your teeth and you swallow it. You suck so much of it into your lungs that until you die you never stop spitting up coal dust. Some of you cough so hard that you wonder if you have a lung left. Slowly you notice you are getting short of breath when you walk up a hill. On the job, you stop more often to catch your breath. Finally, just walking across the room at home is an effort because it makes you so short of breath. This is what I'm here to talk about.

Coal workers' pneumoconiosis is the most important occupational dust disease occurring in the United States today.

—DR. LORIN E. KERR,
speaking at a UMWA convention in 1968

Forty-two years I lived in one little town, Chattaroy. We had to work for eighteen and twenty hours a day and use an old breast auger. We'd drill up a hole, snub a place, load up the dust, shoot the middle hole, and snuff bad iron smoke all day long.

—NIMROD WORKMAN

Jim Hamilton speaks out for black lung benefits at the Survival March on Washington.

The black lung movement started in 1965 in Pennsylvania. That was the first state to get legislation passed and to get compensation for sick miners.

In West Virginia, Donald Rasmussen was the one who started the research and testing of miners. He and others began to tour the country, informing miners what was really happening to them. They weren't dying of "miner's asthma," but rather pneumoconiosis, or black lung, which was destroying the air sacs in their lungs. We felt the need of an organization that would push for legislation in the states that didn't have a black lung law.

Arnold Miller and others formed the Black Lung Association in West Virginia, and we got a group going in Kentucky.

—BILL WORTHINGTON

Doug Yarrow

In the autumn of 1968 a delegation of miners came to see me and asked would I be willing to come and speak for them and with them about this problem. I agreed.

At this point there had been very little education and dissemination of information on the problem. I was introduced to I. E. Buff. Dr. Buff deserves a great deal of credit for getting recognition for the problems of lung disease in coal miners. He is responsible for much of the compensation and health and safety legislation that's been passed.

Initially both Dr. Buff and I received a lot of criticism from the medical profession in West Virginia. I think by now most of the medical people are in agreement with us.

—DONALD RASMUSSEN

In 1969, 40,000 West Virginia miners walked off their jobs in a wildcat strike to support legislation drafted by the newly formed Black Lung Association. The union ordered them back to work. They refused, and when hundreds of them marched by union headquarters in Charleston, they booed and raised their clenched fists in anger. . . . Finally, after the strike had continued three weeks, legislators . . . passed a bill that made it possible for black lung victims to receive assistance under the state's workmen's-compensation laws. Said Dr. Buff: "I think there is going to be an entire change in the state. For the first time the ordinary coal miner is free. Now he knows what he can do when he joins with other miners."

—BILL PETERSON

The National Coal Mine Health and Safety Law read so good that we thought it would solve our problems. But in the end, Congress passed a generality and left the specifics—the rules and regulations—up to the Social Security Administration. And we were to find out as time went on that our problems weren't over. The act wasn't being carried out properly, especially in West Virginia and Kentucky.

We had formed chapters around the region and we began to get together to talk about these things. We had some help to draw up an amendment to the 1969 Health and Safety Act. In order to get that passed, we had to threaten another strike. I remember at that time the president was planning a trip to Russia. So we wrote him that if he didn't sign this bill and went on off to Russia, he wouldn't have no air conditioning at the White House when he got back—or any lights to land at the airport with either. We forced him to sign that bill.

We're still in a hassle to be sure the intent of Congress is carried out. It's been a constant battle—a seven-days-a-week, year-after-year fight—just to keep the program working according to law.

—BILL WORTHINGTON

Now I see my battle's just still goin'. I have to fight right on as long as there's breath in me. So I've started to organize my people in this county to get together and fight for our rights. . . .

We're entitled to this lung-disease pay. I've worked under them hazardous times and I'm a sick man; I've got lung disease that I got from coal dust and rock dust . . . like all the rest of these old coal miners that's signed up for this black lung, that's entitled to it and been turned down.

—JIM HAMILTON

NOTICE TO ALL COAL MINERS THAT HAVE BEEN TURNED DOWN FOR BLACK LUNG BENEFITS

I am on the move to organize the poor people of this community. Let's let our state and federal governments know we are on the map and we will not back down. There has been a lot of us old coal miners that have been turned down for the Black Lung Benefits by some dumb-head doctors who don't know our conditions—been picked by our compensation boards and don't know how to read X-rays. We have worked in the underground coal mines and we are smothering to death with this disease caused by working in coal dust, rock dust, and bad air for forty to fifty years.

Let's stand together and show these dumb-heads that we will not be treated like this. We will march and we will fight for our rights. Let's move and go together. That is the way I led the coal miners to victory in 1933 and 1934. I am in this battle to win.

—JIM HAMILTON,
Pike County, Kentucky

BLACK LUNG PAYCHECK

WORDS: WALTER BROCK
(DONE IN TALKING BLUES STYLE)

I worked in a coal mine for twenty-three year.
Seems to me I breathed enough bad air
To kill me and three or four more.
But I'm gonna get my black lung pension
And that's for sure.
'Cause I coughed all night last night
And the night before.

I said, woman, I believe I'll walk off
Down about the store.
I got down there and I bought a jar of coffee.
I said, Merchant, I would buy more
If you'll wait on me
'Til I get my black lung pension.
I said, I'm gonna get it
And that's for sure.
'Cause I coughed all night last night
And the night before.

I come back home
And I got mad and I walked the floor.
I said, woman, when I get my black lung pension
Remind me to trade at another store.
I said, I'm gonna get it
And that's for sure.
'Cause I coughed all night last night
And the night before.

I get up early every morning.
I don't know how many trips I make to the door,
Runnin', peepin', lookin'
To see if that mailboy
Is gonna bring my black lung check up to the door.
When he don't bring it
I say, woman, we just have to wait a little more,
But I'm gonna get it
And that's for sure.
'Cause I coughed all night last night
And the night before.

One mornin' the mailboy pulled up to my door
Read me a notice to go back to the doctor once more
To see if I had the black lung for sure.
I went back there for a breathin' test,
And that lady stood up there.
She just kept on hollerin'
More and more and more.
I got done, I said, listen here, lady,
I'm gonna get that black lung pension
And that's for sure.
'Cause I coughed all night last night
And the night before.

I done waited eleven months
And just a little more.
I done wore out one knob on my door,
Runnin', peepin', and lookin'
To see if that mailboy is gonna bring my black lung check
Up to my door.
I says, I'm gonna get it
And that's for sure.
'Cause I coughed all night last night
And the night before.

© 1975 by Walter Brock

It came as a great shock to me in 1968 and 1969 to learn that our efforts were not only opposed by the coal industry, but also by the leadership in the United Mine Workers union. Not only did they lobby behind the scenes in the state legislature, but they actually threatened members of the Black Lung Association who were pushing the struggle.

Tony Boyle was opposed to compensation for coal miners in the 1969 act—or even including the issue of health into the national legislation—on grounds that the "health issue was just too complicated and required more research."

What the . . . black lung movement did was to point out the failure of United Mine Workers' hierarchy to really support the rank-and-file miners. In West Virginia it was the turning point. Once the movement got going, the miners saw clearly that their union leaders were not supporting them.

—DONALD RASMUSSEN

REFORM IN THE UNITED MINE WORKERS

The Union that once protected the men from the bosses now protects the bosses from the men.

—*campaign statement by*
ARNOLD MILLER,
Summer, 1972

Reform slate candidates Harry Patrick, Arnold Miller, Mike Trbovich for leadership of the United Mine Workers of America.

Tony Boyle campaigns.

Coal miners don't need to be talked *at*, they need to be talked *with*. We need to derive strength from each other, and in this way, we can correct all the problems that confront this great union. . . . We've got a lot of work to do in order to bring this union to the place it should be!

—JOSEPH YABLONSKI

To the men of the United Mine Workers of America, I am pleading with you to stop and take a look at what the International and District and some local union presidents are doing to our union. The International President, Tony Boyle, and district officials of Districts 29 and 17 are breaking our union! They are forcing you to work under any kind of conditions, but let me plead with you union men that are left: get rid of these men.

Set your union up so you can elect your union officials, international, district, retirement board officials and local union officers. Get rid of the dirty things that are going on in our union today.

If you get hurt and try to get your compensation, the coal company lawyers and doctor will beat you out of your money if they can.

If you get rock dust or black lung, you are lucky if you get one-half of what is coming to you. You go to what is called a union lawyer, which you pay. They will tell you to take whatever they offer you.

Tony Boyle and the officials of Districts 29 and 17 are no good. Let's organize our union and do something about this before it is too late. I will help in any way I can.

—LEWIS COLEMAN,
disabled miner,
Maben, West Virginia

The miners' struggle to clear out the Boyle regime and clean up the union leadership began formally in 1969. Joseph Yablonski declared his candidacy for the presidency on May 29. He ended his speech with a prophetic statement: "I'm not naïve enough to think that there won't be much difficulty and I know the lengths they will go to."

After a summer of campaigning, the election was held December 9. Official returns showed that Boyle had won by 34,504 votes, almost a 2-to-1 margin. Yablonski had done well only where he had poll watchers.

Even though he had lost the election, Yablonski had no intention of giving up his fight with the Boyle administration.

Tony Boyle stole the election . . . his campaign can best be described as a great treasury raid in which he converted the dues of honest mine workers and elderly pensioners to his personal campaign and used the personnel of the UMW as though they were his private servants.

I've taken Boyle to court before, and I'll take him there again. And next time he'll go to jail, where the hell he belongs.

Maybe we lost the skirmish—but we're still gonna win the war! We haven't given up! We're gonna fight this thing all the way. . . .

—JOSEPH YABLONSKI

Joseph Yablonski talks with miners during the 1969 UMWA campaign.

Jeanne M. Rasmussen

Shortly after one o'clock on the morning of December 31, 1969, Joseph Yablonski, his wife, Margaret, and his daughter Charlotte were murdered in their beds—shot to death by three men.

. . . When I went home for the last time I was shocked to walk into my parents' bedroom and see three guns lined up on the walls and on the window sills; to know the way my father abhorred guns, wouldn't have them in the house; to see our home an armed camp; to know the reign of terror under which he was living at that time, after the election.

I couldn't comprehend the full scope of it then; I can now, because I was raised by a good man who told me, "Keep guns out of your house. Your children won't be hurt. You can protect yourself."

But yet he had to bring guns into his home he was so terrified. And now, in the wake of his death and the murder of my mother and sister, I, who would never have a gun in my home, go to sleep each night, a loaded pistol under my pillow, and my wife tosses and turns.

I know the thousands of people who supported my father are living under that same reign of terror. They feel, as I feel, that unless the government of the United States, whether it be the Secretary of Labor, the Department of Justice, the U.S. Senate, or the combined will of them all, gets to the roots of the corruption and tyranny in the United Mine Workers union, they won't sleep well.

—JOSEPH A. "CHIP" YABLONSKI

At the time of publication, nine people have been convicted of, or have pleaded guilty to, these murders, including UMWA officials Silous Huddleston, William Prater, Albert Pass, and William Turnblazer. On September 6, 1973, Tony Boyle was charged with ordering and planning the murder. Before he could be brought to trial, he attempted to take his own life. In April, 1974, he was convicted and sentenced to life in prison.

Joseph Yablonski's funeral

THE YABLONSKI MURDER

WORDS AND MUSIC: HAZEL DICKENS

Clarksville, Pennsylvania, is not too far from here.
Coal miners were hoping for a brighter new year.
But for Jock Yablonski, his daughter and wife,
The new year brought an ending to their precious life.
  Well it's cold-blooded murder, friends, I'm talking about.
  Now, who's gonna stand up and who's gonna fight?
  You better clean up that union, put it on solid ground,
  And get rid of that dirty trash keeps the working man down.

Well death bells were ringing, Jock knew very well
They had stolen union money and Jock just had to tell.
Because he wouldn't take part in all their dirty plans
He paid with his life to help the working man.
  Well it's cold-blooded murder, etc.

Now Jock Yablonski was a coal miner's friend,
He fought for the rights of all working men.
He begged the law to protect him but they turned him down.
Now Jock, his wife and daughter all lay beneath the ground.
  Well it's cold-blooded murder, etc.

Oh, Lord, the poor miner, will his fight never end?
They'll abuse, even murder him to further their plans.
Oh, where is his victory, how will it stand?
It'll stand when poor working men all join hands.
  Well it's cold-blooded murder, etc.

Tony Boyle taken to court for indictment in the murders

The reform movement within the United Mine Workers did not die with Jock Yablonski. His supporters went on to form Miners For Democracy and in 1972, the Memorial Day weekend, they held a convention in Wheeling, West Virginia, to nominate a slate of candidates to challenge Tony Boyle in the upcoming UMW elections. (The 1969 election had been overturned for massive vote fraud and intimidation.) Arnold Miller, a soft-spoken, disabled miner serving as president of the Black Lung Association, was nominated for the presidency. Yablonski campaign manager Mike Trbovich and 1971 contract strike leader Harry Patrick completed the slate.

—THOMAS N. BETHELL

Arnold Miller talking to miners

Earl Dotter

Granny Hager

We fought to get the union. But the leaders of our union has let the old coal miners down. They're fixin' to let the young ones down. They're gonna fall harder than the old ones if they don't begin to tighten up on the thing and put the union where it ought to be. The union don't belong up in Washington. We ain't got any coal mines up there.

Anybody that goes to Washington—let it be the man they got there, let it be Miller, or let it be me, or any other man—the local unions voted on a man and sent him up to Washington, they only sent him up there to kind of lead the thing. The local unions are supposed to vote on the kinds of things that they want and that they need. Then the man they've got up there as president, he's supposed to back the locals up and these men to get just exactly what they have labored for and what they've worked for.

I'm just as strong a union man. And I'll stand by the obligation I took. I'll go a hundred miles or more out of my way right now to help another union man.

You know what I call a union man? A man that'll get up and go to his brother and stand by him according to his obligation and stay with him and his family till the hair flies . . . until the hide slips. Brother, then you've got a union man.

—NIMROD WORKMAN

195

The voting began December 1, ended December 8. Teams of specially trained Labor Department supervisors kept watch at every polling place. In sealed boxes, the ballots were moved under guard to Labor Department offices in Washington. The counting began December 12, closely scrutinized by around-the-clock observers from both sides. The Labor Department had figured the counting would take 4 or 5 days. Suprisingly, however, the outcome was clear within 36 hours; by the evening of December 13 Miller was leading with a comfortable 53% margin that grew steadily from then on.

Picking an apt figure of speech, an unidentified Boyle aide told a wire service reporter that "we're going down the drain."

The final count was Miller 70,373, Boyle 56,334.

—THOMAS N. BETHELL

The Labor Department certified Miller's election December 20; and two days later the election was made official.

Miller walked across the grass and through the open doors of the Mine Workers' Building, across the lobby, past a large glowering bust of John L., and down a flight of steps to the large basement room where the inauguration was to take place. Suddenly there was pandemonium—hundreds of miners jumping to their feet, cheering, singing, yelling, crying. Miller, who is normally the most composed of men, found himself moist-eyed and turned away, embarrassed. But there was nothing to be embarrassed about. It was a moment of glory.

—THOMAS N. BETHELL

BETTER TIMES WILL SOON BE COMING TO THE HILLS

BASED ON THE STATE ANTHEM OF WEST VIRGINIA

Oh those West Vir-gin-ia hills, so mag – ni-fi-cent, so grand With their peo – ple stand-ing faith-ful, as all West Virginians can Is it a – ny won-der, then, that my heart with rap-ture thrills For better times will soon be coming to those West Vir-gin-ia hills. Ov-er the hills,_____ beau-ti-ful hills,_____ There's been hard times in the West Vir-gin-ia hills_____ But if we all u – ni-ted stand and you

take your bro-ther's hand Bet-ter times will soon be com-ing to the hills._____ Oh those hills_____

These verses were sung as parody of the state anthem in the West Virginia coal fields in the early 1930s.

Oh those West Virginia hills, so majestic and so grand,
With their miners standing loyal as all union men should stand,
Is it any wonder then that my heart with rapture thrills
For again we have a union in the West Virginia hills.

Oh those West Virginia hills, they're so beautiful and green
If they could only tell you of the awful sights they've seen
Of their union sons and daughters, so noble and so brave,
By a cruel gunman's bullet gone to fill an early grave.

The following version was written by Michael Kline in the late 1960s.

Oh those West Virginia hills, so magnificent, so grand
With their people standing faithful, as all West Virginians can
Is it any wonder, then, that my heart with rapture thrills
For better times will soon be coming to those West Virginia hills.
    Over the hills, beautiful hills,
    There's been hard times in the West Virginia hills
    But if we all united stand and you take your brother's hand
    Better times will soon be coming to the hills.

Oh those East Kentucky hills, so beautiful, so green
If they could only tell you of the awful times they've seen
Gutted roads and worn out schools, and they treat your kids like fools
There's been hard times in the East Kentucky hills.
    Over the hills, beautiful hills,
    There's been hard times in the East Kentucky hills, etc.

Oh those Appalachian hills, so rugged and so dear
For generations ruled through corruption, greed and fear,
Those that couldn't take a stand, they were driven from the land
And the strippers scarred those Appalachian hills.
    Over the hills, beautiful hills,
    There's been hard times in the Appalachian hills, etc.

© 1975 *by Michael Kline* (words)

The rank and file have now found a voice. We're not going to stop there. We're going to fight right on and help keep this union what it ought to be.

The old spirit will come back. The union will be great again.

—BILL WORTHINGTON

I'm 23. When I first got my job at the mine 4 years ago, I found a lot of problems. The company wouldn't follow the contract and didn't give a damn about our safety as long as that coal was coming out. The local leaders were all older guys, all buddies with the district and Tony Boyle.

For the first year, I didn't go to local meetings, but I did begin to realize that there were a lot of guys, especially young boys, who had grievances like I did. Finally, a group of us got together and decided to go to meetings and learn about the contract.

It was hard to get through. The officers didn't like us young guys rocking the boat. They called us "radicals" and really tried to discourage us from taking part in our own union.

The Yablonski campaign and the black lung marches gave me some hope, and we kept working at our local. At our last election, I got elected to the mine committee which gave me a chance to butt heads with the company on these problems.

When this election came, we had a meeting of guys in district 17 with Arnold Miller. He said we needed an observer in the district office. I was really surprised when he asked me to take the job. I expected it would be one of the older men. But Arnold was serious about giving young guys a chance.

I've seen a lot in this job since then. I saw how little the District men do for the men. They gave me a hard time and threatened me. They told me if we lost I'd better find a new home. It really burned me up to think these guys would be retiring on $500 a month and up.

After Arnold won, I was set to go back to the mine, but they asked me to stay as a monitor until the men in the district can elect their officers.

I feel now that I can always be involved in the union. I look forward to when they move the headquarters to the coal fields, because I think then the UMW will be able to be a voice on all kinds of problems.

What I've learned in this campaign will be important to me for a lifetime. So will the friends I've made. Before, I had never been out of this area. Now, I can go anywhere in southern West Virginia and have dinner with friends. Things have changed a lot for this union and this state. And things have changed a lot for me.

—EDDIE BURKE

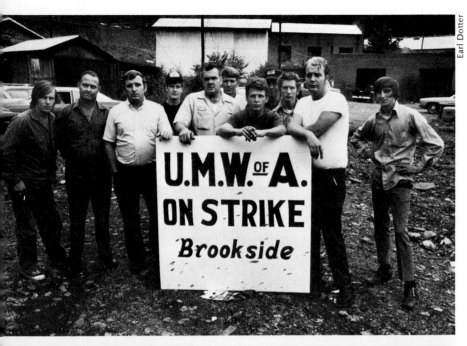

Earl Dotter

Earl Dotter

We've learned to say "No!" At Duke's Brookside mine we're out on strike. No contract, no work. No protection, no coal. We don't want to shut off anybody's lights. But we can't let Duke Power run our lives the way Duke runs its mines.

Since the election of the reform candidates, the UMWA has come back to life organizing miners in the mountains. In Harlan County, Kentucky, in the tiny community of Brookside, the miners and their families have taken on the Duke Power Company.

In July they voted out the Southern Labor Union and chose as their representatives the new, reform leadership of the UMWA. Now the 180 coal miners at the Brookside mine are on strike in hopes of winning a UMWA contract from the company. Their wives, their children, and retired miners have all been jailed along with the strikers for lending support to the strike.

They're not making any outrageous demands. In return for doing the most dangerous work in America, they want fair pay, safer working conditions, decent medical benefits, and the right to a UMWA Safety Committee.

The miners believe they will win.

"With so many young men, and the backing of the United Mine Workers the way they've come through, and Duke Power being rich enough to settle with us,* I think we will win," striker Jerry Johnson said. "Anyway, when you've got nothing to start with, you've got nothing to lose. And we've seen too much hell in Harlan not to fight this as hard and as long as it takes to win."

—*from the UMWA Journal*

---

* Duke Power Company is the sixth largest privately owned power company in the world. Their profits last year exceeded $90 million.

The miners at Brookside have been out on strike for more than a year. There have been violence against and harassment of the strikers and their wives. Kentucky State Police were sent in during the summer of 1974 to help the company drive to break the strike. Those on strike are equally determined. They feel they must win the strike or be driven out, and they are determined not to leave.

Throughout our lives and the lives of our fathers and grandfathers before us, companies like Duke Power have come into these mountains looking for wealth and riches.

Isolated from the rest of the country, we in these mountains fought back as best we can. But we faced multimillion dollar corporations that held a stranglehold over our lives and our land. . . .

All our lives we've known companies like Duke Power which buy up a coal camp community like Brookside and think they've bought the lives of the people who live there as well.

—DARRELL DEATON
Vice-President
UMWA Local at Brookside

I have talked to a lot of old people—pensioners and coal miners, and we don't want this stuff. Why don't they set down and talk with us, and get this over with, and we will go back to work. We are working people. We are not outlaws and don't want no handout. We just want to make a decent living. We just want decent wages, and want decent safety conditions and we don't want this violence.

—JAMES TURNER

My sole purpose in being there is to help the coal miner. My father was a coal miner, I've got two brothers who are coal miners, and my husband is a coal miner; and I know what coal miners go through with. I have lived through it and I was born and raised in it, but when a judge puts three men on a picket line—three pickets—and lets them scabs come in and spit in their face and make obscene gestures at them and everything else, and those men have to sit there and take it, then it is time for the women to step in.

We knew there would be more violence. We knew if the women didn't come in there would be violence, because the men were getting fed up to their teeth with this. So the women came in. The women all went down there . . . and the scabs were taking pictures and the women whipped them.

—LOIS SCOTT

Earl Dotter

On August 29, 1974, the Brookside strike was settled with an agreement between the UMWA and Duke Power Company. The settlement followed the shooting and subsequent death of a young Brookside striker, Lawrence Jones, by an Eastover foreman. It also came just a few days after a massive march and rally in Harlan which brought together UMWA miners and supporters from all across the country.

Nine days later a second UMWA contract was signed at the nearby Pathfork-Harlan mine.

"The dominoes are beginning to fall in Eastern Kentucky. First Brookside, then—Pathfork-Harlan. There will be many more UMW mines to follow in Eastern Kentucky and throughout the coalfields."

—HARRY PATRICK,
UMWA Secretary-Treasurer

"This strike brought us together. It taught us who the real enemy is, and it showed us that we can fight back and win, if we're organized."

—JERRY JOHNSON,
Brookside miner

WHICH SIDE ARE YOU ON?
(updated)

Which side are you on, now?
Which side are you on?
Which side are you on?
Which side are you on?

The miners on the picket line
Have Eastover on the run
Until they sign with the union
They will not mine a ton.

The miners down at Brookside
Are a courageous bunch of men
And with their women by their sides
Each has the strength of ten.

Duke Power thought they'd win this strike
With the miners in misery
But the union will shove it down Duke's throat
With a miner's victory.

Which side are you on, now?
Which side are you on?
Which side are you on?
Which side are you on?

Tennessee farmer

BETTER LISTEN TO THE VOICES FROM THE MOUNTAINS

It is difficult for the people of Appalachia to speak collectively and to be heard. We have no advocates, no churchmen, no elected representatives to speak for us. As social units, these groups are more apt to speak against us. We must, therefore, understand that we will only be heard by American society and even by our fellows in Appalachia as we find the means and, God willing, the courage to speak as a united people.

—WARREN WRIGHT

VOICES FROM THE MOUNTAINS

WORDS AND MUSIC: RUTHIE GORTON

(FREELY)

You'd bet-ter lis-ten___ to the voi-ces from the moun-tains___ Try-in' to tell___ you what you just might need to know, 'Cause the em-pire's days are num-bered if you're coun-___tin'___ And the peo-ple just get stron-___ger blow by blow. 2.

© 1975 by Ruthie Gordon

You'd better listen to the voices from the mountains
Tryin' to tell you what you just might need to know,
'Cause the empire's days are numbered if you're countin'
And the people just get stronger blow by blow.

You'd better listen when they talk about strip mining
Gonna turn the rollin' hills to acid clay.
If you're preachin' all about that silver lining,
You'll be talkin' till the hills are stripped away.

You'd better listen to the cries of the dyin' miners,
Better feel the pain of their children and their wives.
We gotta stand and fight together for survival,
And it's bound to mean a change in all our lives.

In explosions or from Black Lung they'll be dyin',
And the operator's guilty of this crime.
But the killin' won't be stopped by all your cryin'.
We gotta fight for what we need, let's seize the time.

You'd better listen to the voices from the mountains
Tryin' to tell you what you just might need to know,
'Cause the empire's days are numbered if you're countin'
And the people just get stronger blow by blow.

With all the emphasis at my command, I report that a revolution is brewing in Appalachia. The people are not going to stand by any longer while strip miners rip up their homeland. The people have been waiting with rising impatience for Congress to act to stop this wholesale destruction of the forests, soil, hills, streams, and the homes of the people. If Congress just passes one of these innocuous bills* designed to quiet the public outcry while meeting the demands of the National Coal Association and the American Mining Congress, there'll be a Boston Tea Party which won't be a tea party.

—REP. KEN HECHLER

*Just such an innocuous bill was passed by Congress in December 1974, only to be pocket vetoed by President Ford.

207

I've been working on this for years and I can't come up with anything but people to stop a strip mine. That's the only thing that's ever stopped one. I think if there's enough people you can do anything.

I've not seen a strip operator that's not scared. He's scared when he first sets foot on that mountain. He don't know what opposition he's going to run into. They put their little scouts out to see who comes up the hill, and who does this and that. Now they're scared. They know most people is against it. Most people don't want those rocks and mud sliding off in their gardens and behind their houses and on the road. . . .

I think if you had something that said "union"—a people's union—it would be more effective on a strip operation. They'd think twice. They'd think, "How many people is that going to be? . . . A union could be thousands of people, and we better think twice before we shoot at one of them or start any violence, because we could just get wiped out."

. . . It's time we do something that we can work with in the future. I think we'll either have to move in this direction or shut up and hush. I don't know any other tool to fight 'em with. I think we've tried everything else. I don't know nothing else to use on 'em but people.

—EULA HALL

With the cutbacks in federal funds, the movement's going to be more widespread than it was in the '60s, and it's going to be well organized. More grass-roots leaders will emerge. It's not going to be confined to just east Kentucky or West Virginia. I believe it's going to be a coalition of people moving in unity.

As I go around, I get the feelings of a lot of people—especially the feelings of the young people and how discouraged they're becoming. They don't really understand what's behind it yet, but they're mad. I think it's a healthy sign.

We're going to have to stay loose and change as the people change if we want to be involved. And I know I will be involved. I've worked too long to see something start to happen and then quit. I'm not about to.

—BUCK MAGGARD

People are not going to sit down and starve to death and let their kids starve to death. If there's anything to eat, they're going to eat it—if they have to take it; any way they can get it.

They won't have to go to Vietnam to fight their guerrilla warfare—it'll be right here in eastern Kentucky. These mountains is a good place for guerrilla warfare—they've got it dug full of holes already.

—EVERETTE THARP

There's not just one group of oppressed people in the mountains. We've got miners, we've got welfare recipients, we've got blacks, Indians, we've got the whole works. But the government until now has kept those groups fighting each other till they never had time to fight the oppressor. And hopefully at least Appalachia is waking up to the fact that there's oppression across state lines—and across group lines.

I don't know. How do you get people to understand that you don't have to sit there and take it, that you can stand up and fight it?

It has to start somewhere. Mountain people move maybe a little slower than people in the cities would, but once they get to moving it's like a giant steam-roller. They knock down everything in their path. And I think it can happen. I think the mountain people are going to wake up to the fact that they've got a lot of cleaning out to do. And when they get through, there aren't going to be very many crooked politicians left.

—SHELVA THOMPSON

I'm sick of these things—telegrams of condolence, letters from people saying they're sorry—I'm sick of it. There's just too much plain, ordinary irresponsibility in the coal industry, and the former leadership of this union has been too close to the industry to see it or fight it. That's over now.

I have seen more than my share of needless suffering in my lifetime, but I have never before been in a position to do very much to stop it. Now that has changed, and I want you to know there will be no peace in the coal industry until this bloodshed ends.

—ARNOLD MILLER

Land developments, resorts, etc., have driven the price of marginal farm and timber land from a low of $100 an acre to a whopping $1000 an acre in a half decade. So high has the price and taxation on mountain land become in the last few years, that the dream of a mountain farmer to have at least one son stay home to till the soil has changed to the nightmare that he may not even be able to maintain the farm for his own retirement. . . .

. . . The giant holdings of the corporations in Appalachia should be federalized and homesteaded just like the U.S. Government seized and homesteaded in the West. If we can do this to the poor Indians, there is no reason why we can-

not do it to the rich corporations. This would simply be returning to the mountaineers the timber and land that they were swindled out of at the turn of the century.

Resort complexes that serve only middle-class skiers and other kinds of intruders into the mountains should be prohibited. They bring only crime, high prices, and disrespect for mountaineers with them to the mountains. Folks migrating to northern cities know that mountaineers are not welcome in the rich suburbs, so there is no reason for us to make the suburbanites welcome in the mountains.

—JAMES BRANSCOME

Phil Primack

Kris Mendenhall

Don West, Pipestem,
West Virginia

We need to be skeptical, to be suspicious, to ask a million questions, and to demand answers of all who would come to save us, no matter what cloak they wear. Had we asked the right questions and insisted upon the right answers at the right time, we might have been saved from a TVA that devastates an entire area for its strip coal; from a Corps of Engineers that builds dams simply to build dams; from a Forest Service that serves only the lumber industry; from an Appalachian Regional Commission that seeks not to assist, but to eliminate an entire culture rich in its own heritage. We might even have been saved from our own folly in turning over the greatest wealth in the nation to a few moneymen from the outside who wanted our minerals.

We don't need any new ideology forced upon us. We just need help in seeing and understanding all the alternatives. Give us all the facts—and I mean all of them—and we will make the right decisions.

—TOM GISH

NEW DAY COMIN'

WORDS AND MUSIC: ANNE HOPKINS

Go-in' on down that new road, New road, new road,
Go-in' on down that new road, There's a new day—com-in' to the
hills. There's a new day com-in', sis-ter, There's a
new day com-in', bro-ther,—When we'll all stand together, There's a
new day—— com-in' to the hills.
There's a day a-com-in' When earth will not be torn And the
migh-ty rich-es deep with in Are once a-gain our own.
We'll take back our land, our pride, No more in pov-er-ty,
Moun-tain wo-men, moun-tain men, To-ge-ther stand-ing free.

© 1975 Anne Hopkins

Goin' on down that new road,
New road, new road,
Goin' on down that new road,
There's a new day comin' to the hills.

There's a new day comin', sister,
There's a new day comin', brother,
When we'll all stand together,
There's a new day comin' to the hills.

There's a day a-comin'
When the earth will not be torn
And the mighty riches deep within
Are once again our own.
We'll take back our land, our pride,
No more in poverty,
Mountain women, mountain men,
Together standing free.

Goin' on down that new road,
New road, new road,
Goin' on down that new road,
There's a new day comin' to the hills.

The morning sky is fresh and clean,
The streams are running clear,
Corn is growing straight and tall
High up on the hill.
Laughing children sing and play,
Run down the mountainside,
No longer growing up to leave
With hunger in their eyes.

Goin' on down that new road,
New road, new road,
Goin' on down that new road,
There's a new day comin' to the hills.

There's a new day comin', sister,
There's a new day comin', brother,
When we'll all stand together,
There's a new day comin' to the hills.

BRIGHT MORNING STARS

WORDS AND MUSIC: TRADITIONAL
AS SUNG BY GEORGE TUCKER

Bright morning stars are rising,
Bright morning stars are rising,
Bright morning stars are rising,
Day is a-breakin' in my soul.

Oh, where are our dear fathers,
Oh, where are our dear fathers,
Oh, where are our dear fathers,
Day is a-breakin' in my soul.

They are down in the valley praying,
They are down in the valley praying,
They are down in the valley praying,
Day is a-breakin' in my soul.

   Bright morning stars are rising, etc.

Oh, where are our dear mothers,
Oh, where are our dear mothers,
Oh, where are our dear mothers,
Day is a-breakin' in my soul.

They have gone to heaven a-shouting,
They have gone to heaven a-shouting,
They have gone to heaven a-shouting,
Day is a-breakin' in my soul.

   Bright morning stars are rising, etc.

I CAN FEEL THE SWEET WINDS BLOWING

BILL STAINES is a northern song writer who spends time in Appalachia.

JOAN BOYD is a Tennessee singer and song writer, known for her songs about life in Appalachia. She now lives in Knoxville, Tennessee.

EVERETTE THARP, a retired coal miner and local union organizer, is a leader in poor people's struggles in central Appalachia. He helped start the Appalachian Committee for Full Employment in Hazard, Kentucky, and surrounding communities and was active in the War on Poverty. He lives in Perry County, Kentucky.

HAZEL DICKENS is a prolific song writer and singer from West Virginia. Many of her relatives have worked in the mines. She now lives in Washington, D.C.

HARRIETTE SIMPSON ARNOW is the author of numerous books on Appalachia. She is presently living in Michigan.

MIKE SMATHERS is a native of Big Lick, Tennessee, and has been a pastor and teacher. He currently works for the Center for Community Change, Washington, D.C., as coordinator of a mountain community education program.

BILLY EDD WHEELER, poet and playwright, singer and song writer, has written many songs about Appalachia. A native of West Virginia, he is presently living in Swannanoa, North Carolina.

CHAPTER I

GEORGE TUCKER is a former miner and an active community leader from Beaver, Kentucky, known for his humorous songs and stories and his knowledge of mountain folk songs, ballads, and hymns.

REP. KEN HECHLER, of West Virginia, "the coal miner's congressman," has long been a foe of strip mining and an advocate of strong laws governing mine health and safety for the coal industry.

THOMAS N. BETHELL, a writer-photographer, started *Coal Patrol*, a muckraking periodical on the coal industry. He is now the director of research for the United Mine Workers of America.

WARREN WRIGHT, farmer, mechanic, preacher, former executive director of the Council of the Southern Mountains (a regional organization of grass-roots activists), and a strong foe of strip mining, is a native of Letcher County, Kentucky. He is now developing a research center on his farm.

JOHN TILLER, a former coal miner from Trammel, Virginia, is currently on the staff of the Council of the Southern Mountains.

JEAN RITCHIE, from Viper, Kentucky, is known around the world for her traditional and contemporary songs. She lives in New York and performs widely both in this country and abroad.

J. T. BEGLEY, a native of Blackey, Kentucky, is a lawyer for the Appalachian Research and Defense Fund in Lexington, Kentucky.

JIM GARLAND was a local union organizer and song maker in the Kentucky coal mines during the 1930s. He now lives on the West Coast.

MIKE CLARK is the director of the Highlander Research and Education Center. A native of North Carolina, he has been active for several years in various struggles around the mountains.

MICHAEL KLINE, a singer and song writer, now lives in West Virginia. He was an active participant in community organizing during the heyday of the War on Poverty and was responsible for many of the satirical songs that emerged.

JAMES BRANSCOME, from Virginia, has worked for the Appalachian Regional Commission and was a director of Save Our Kentucky, an anti-strip-mining organization. He is presently on the staff of the Highlander Research and Education Center.

JOHN PRINE is a young song writer from Chicago with a growing national reputation. His parents are from Kentucky.

WENDELL BERRY is a teacher, farmer, and writer. He teaches English at the University of Kentucky, Lexington.

BILL CHRISTOPHER is from Petros, Tennessee. He is a singer and song writer and an active member of SOCM (Save Our Cumberland Mountains), a strong grass-roots organization opposing strip mining.

JOE BEGLEY is an active community leader and foe of strip mining in Blackey, Kentucky.

GURNEY NORMAN is a writer from Perry County, Kentucky, who now lives in California but spends much of his time in Appalachia.

JOE MULLOY, now a resident of West Virginia, worked for the Appalachian Volunteers in east Kentucky until he was arrested for organizing against strip mining in 1967. Charges of sedition against him and several co-workers were later dropped. He has also worked for the Southern Conference Educational Fund in the mountains.

JIM W. MILLER, a writer-poet, teaches at Western State University, Bowling Green, Kentucky.

HARRY CAUDILL is an attorney in Whitesburg, Kentucky, and the author of two well-known books on Appalachia.

EULA HALL is a vigorous community worker and leader from Craynor, Kentucky. She is one of the mainstays in the East Kentucky Welfare Rights Organization and the Mud Creek Health Clinic, and is currently president of the Kentucky Black Lung Association.

BESSIE SMITH GAYHEART is an active and vocal opponent of strip mining in Appalachia. She has led many public protests against strip mining, including a demonstration by women members of the Appalachian Group to Save the Land and People, which stopped strip mining in one section of Knott County, Kentucky.

CHAPTER II

JOHN ARMS is a young east Kentuckian who has taken part in community organization programs since he was fifteen.

TOM DUFF is a native of Harlan County, Kentucky, who moved north to find work. He testified at the Kennedy Hearings in 1968.

BRUCE PHILLIPS is a song writer and singer from the Southwest who documents contemporary events and cultural moods across the country.

SALLY WORCESTER, who has worked with community organizations in many areas of Appalachia, is a member of the Women's String Band in Morgantown, West Virginia.

RICH KIRBY, a singer, song writer, and community worker, has been active in mountain organizations for a number of years.

DOUG YOUNGBLOOD is a poet, musician, and writer from Chicago's Uptown district. He runs cultural programs for Appalachian migrants in Chicago.

SI AND KATHY KAHN came to Appalachia in the 1960s to work with various War on Poverty programs. They have written many songs about the region and collect songs and oral history about the mountains.

JIM CORNETT grew up in Blackey, Kentucky. He writes regularly for the *Mountain Eagle* on contemporary problems in Appalachia. One of more than 2 million mountain migrants, he now lives in Ohio.

CHAPTER III

DON WEST, a poet, educator, minister, and historian, is the director of the Appalachian South Folklife Center in Pipestem, West Virginia.

BUCK MAGGARD, a former coal miner and veteran of poor people's struggles in Kentucky through the 1960s, is on the staff of the Highlander Research and Education Center.

SHELVA THOMPSON has been an active leader in welfare-rights groups and related community organizations for a number of years. She lives in Racine, West Virginia.

EDITH EASTERLING is the director of the Marrowbone Folk School, Poorbottom, Kentucky. She worked with various War on Poverty programs during the 1960s and continues to do educational work in her own community.

CHAPTER IV

TILLMAN CADLE was a local organizer for the National Miners Union and a chapter official for the United Mine Workers of America in Kentucky during the 1920s and '30s. A native of Bell County, Kentucky, he now lives in east Tennessee.

JAKE EASTERLING is a retired coal miner from Poorbottom, Kentucky. He has been an active union man for many years.

JIM HAMILTON is a disabled coal miner from Poorbottom, Kentucky, and has been active in the fight for adequate black lung compensation.

JIM JACKSON is a coal miner from Sandy Ridge, Virginia.

MIKE PAXTON is a song writer and radio disc jockey in Pikeville, Kentucky.

NIMROD WORKMAN is a disabled coal miner from Mingo County, West Virginia. He sings old ballads, hymns, contemporary and protest songs, and many songs of his own.

SARAH OGAN GUNNING is from Knox County, Kentucky, where she lived during the labor wars of the 1920s and '30s. She sings traditional songs and many songs she has written herself. She now lives in Michigan.

FLORENCE REECE lived in Harlan County, Kentucky, during the union wars. Her husband, Sam, was a local organizer for many union struggles. They now live in Knoxville, Tennessee.

MYLES HORTON is the founder and retired director of the Highlander Folk School—now the Highlander Research and Education Center. He has worked with many social movements, including the labor movement and the civil rights movement. He is a native of Tennessee.

CHAPTER V

JOHN L. LEWIS, one of America's most colorful labor leaders, was president of the United Mine Workers of America for many years and was a founder of the Congress of Industrial Organizations.

BEN A. FRANKLIN is a reporter for *The New York Times* who has long been interested in the Appalachian region.

JUDITH ANN HENDERSON is a widow of a miner killed in the Mannington mine disaster in West Virginia.

A. BRITTON HUME wrote *Death and the Mines*, a history of the UMWA. He is an assistant to columnist Jack Anderson.

A. T. COLLINS is the lone survivor of the Hyden mine disaster. He lives near Manchester, Kentucky.

DOUG YARROW is a reporter-photographer in Beckley, West Virginia. He and his wife, Ruth, came to Appalachia in the 1960s to work with War on Poverty programs.

ETHEL BREWSTER and SHELBY STEELE are community workers in West Virginia.

JACK WRIGHT is a singer and song writer from Wise, Virginia. He is presently working with Appalshop, in Whitesburg, Kentucky.

MIKE TRBOVICH, a rank-and-file miner for many years, is now vice-president of the United Mine Workers.

CHAPTER VI

ERIC ANDERSON is a northern song writer who came to Hazard, Kentucky, in the early 1960s with the Committee for Miners.

MALVINA REYNOLDS is a prolific song writer from Berkeley, California, who has written songs about most of the major issues in this country over the last twenty-five years.

TOM PAXTON is a northern folk singer and song writer who visited Hazard during the roving-picket period.

DR. LORIN E. KERR is medical director of the UMWA Welfare and Retirement Fund.

BILL WORTHINGTON, a former miner, is a past president of the Kentucky Black Lung Association.

DR. DONALD RASMUSSEN pioneered in testing and diagnosing black lung problems in West Virginia.

BILL PETERSON is a newspaper reporter who covers the Appalachian region. He writes for the Louisville *Courier-Journal & Times.*

WALTER BROCK is a retired miner living in Manchester, Kentucky.

ARNOLD MILLER, the reform-elected president of the United Mine Workers of America, was president of the West Virginia Black Lung Association for several years.

JOSEPH YABLONSKI, a UMWA district president, challenged Tony Boyle for the UMWA presidency in 1969. He was murdered shortly after he filed law suits charging that the election results were rigged by his opponents.

LEWIS COLEMAN is a disabled miner from Maben, West Virginia.

JOSEPH A. "CHIP" YABLONSKI, JR., a son of Joseph Yablonski, is legal counsel for the UMWA.

EDDIE BURKE is a young miner from West Virginia and is presently on the Washington, D.C., staff of the UMWA.

DARRELL DEATON is the vice-president of the UMWA local at Brookside.

JAMES TURNER is a miner on strike from Brookside.

LOIS SCOTT is a member of the Brookside Women's Club, which is active in the strike.

BETTER LISTEN TO THE VOICES FROM THE MOUNTAINS

RUTHIE GORTON is a singer and song writer from California. Most of her material deals with contemporary social issues and problems.

TOM GISH is editor and publisher of the Whitesburg *Mountain Eagle,* a Kentucky newspaper. Since 1955 his paper has played a major role in directing the public's attention to the problems of central Appalachia as well as in helping to develop a strong sense of local political consciousness and solidarity.

ANNE HOPKINS is a young song writer who lives near Knoxville, Tennessee. She is a native of Virginia.

SELECTED BIBLIOGRAPHY AND DISCOGRAPHY

BOOKS

Appalachian People's History Book. Louisville, Kentucky: Mountain Education Associates, Southern Conference Educational Fund, 1971.

Axlerod, Jim, ed. *Growin' Up Country*. Clintwood, Virginia: Council of the Southern Mountains, 1973.

Caudill, Harry M. *Night Comes to the Cumberlands: Biography of a Depressed Area*. Boston: Little, Brown & Co., 1963.

Dreiser, Theodore, *et al. Harlan Miners Speak: Report on Terrorism in the Kentucky Coal Fields*. New York: Da Capo Press, 1970.

Dykeman, Wilma. *The French Broad*. New York: Rinehart & Company, 1955.

Ford, Thomas A., ed. *The Southern Appalachian Region: A Survey*. Lexington: The University Press of Kentucky, 1962.

Gitlin, Todd, and Nanci Hollander. *Uptown: Poor Whites in Chicago*. New York: Harper & Row, 1970.

Hume, A. Britton. *Death and the Mines: Rebellion and Murder in the UMW*. New York: Grossman Pub. Co., 1971.

Kahn, Kathy. *Hillbilly Women*. Garden City, New York: Doubleday & Co., 1973.

People's Appalachian Research Collective, ed. *Appalachia's People, Problems, Alternatives: An Introductory Social Science Reader*. Morgantown, West Virginia: PARC, 1971.

Perry, Huey. *They'll Cut Off Your Project: A Mingo County Chronicle*. New York: Praeger Publishers, 1972.

Walls, David, and John Stephenson, eds. *Appalachia in the Sixties: Decade of Reawakening*. Lexington: The University Press of Kentucky, 1972.

Wiggington, Eliot, ed. *The Foxfire Book*. Garden City, New York: Doubleday & Co., 1972.

————. *Foxfire 2*. Garden City, New York: Doubleday & Co., 1973.

PERIODICALS

Appalachia. Appalachian Regional Commission, 1666 Connecticut Avenue, N.W., Washington, D.C. 20235.

Foxfire. Rabun Gap–Nacoochee School, Rabun Gap, Georgia 30568.

Mountain Eagle. Box 808, Whitesburg, Kentucky 41858.

Mountain Life and Work. Council of the Southern Mountains, Drawer N, Clintwood, Virginia 24228.

People's Appalachia. People's Appalachian Research Collective, Route 3, Box 355B, Morgantown, West Virginia 36505.

UMW Journal. 900 15th Street, N.W., Washington, D.C. 20005.

FILMS, TAPES, REPRINTS, AND PAMPHLETS

Appalachian Movement Press; pamphlet and reprint list. Box 8074, Huntington, West Virginia 25705.

Appalshop, Inc.; films and video tapes. P.O. Box 743, Whitesburg, Kentucky 41858.

Broadside T.V. and Videomaker; video tapes. 204 E. Watauga, Johnson City, Tennessee 37601.

Council of the Southern Mountains; bibliography and bookstore list. C.P.O. 2307, Berea, Kentucky 40403.

Highlander Center; films and pamphlets. Box 245A, RFD 3, New Market, Tennessee 37820.

L.P. RECORDS

"Come All You Coal Miners," songs by Nimrod Workman, Sarah Gunning, George Tucker, Hazel Dickens. Rounder Records, 186 Willow Avenue, Somerville, Massachusetts 02144.

"Lay Down My Pick and Shovel," Nimrod Workman. Dillons Run Records, Capon Bridge, West Virginia 26711.

"They Can't Put It Back," Rich Kirby and Michael Kline. Dillons Run Records.

"The Poverty War Is Dead," Michael Kline. Dillons Run Records.

"Girl of Constant Sorrow," Sarah Ogan Gunning. Folk Legacy Records, Sharon, Connecticut 06069.

"Aunt Molly Jackson." Rounder Records.

"Hazel & Alice," Hazel Dickens and Alice Gerrard. Rounder Records.

"Old Times and Hard Times," Hedy West. Folk Legacy Records.

"Clear Waters Remembered," Jean Ritchie. Sire/London Records, 539 West 25th Street, New York, New York 10001.

"Mountain Music of Kentucky." Folkways Records, 701 Seventh Avenue, New York, New York 10036.

"Tipple, Loom and Rail," Mike Seeger. Folkways Records.

"When Kentucky Had No Union Men," George Davis. Folkways Records.

BOOKS ABOUT MUSIC AND POETRY

Green, Archie. *Only a Miner*. Urbana: University of Illinois Press, 1972.

Greenway, John. *American Folk Songs of Protest*. Philadelphia: University of Pennsylvania Press, 1953.

Korson, George. *Coal Dust on the Fiddle*. Hatboro, Pennsylvania: Folklore Associates, 1965.

Lomax, Alan, Peter Seeger, and Woody Guthrie. *Hard-Hitting Songs for Hard-Hit People*. New York: Oak Publications, 1967.

West, Don. *O Mountaineers!* Huntington, West Virginia: Appalachian Press, 1974.

I CAN FEEL THE SWEET WINDS BLOWING

1. Everette Tharp, reading from autobiography on which he's working, interview (spring, 1973).
2. Hazel Dickens, "As Country As I Could Sing," *Mountain Life and Work* (Dec., 1972).
3. Harriette Simpson Arnow, *Mountain Path*, Introduction. Council of the Southern Mountains, publishers.
4. Mike Smathers, "Notes of a Native Son," *Mountain Life and Work* (Feb., 1973).
5. Relon Hampton, letter to the *Mountain Eagle* (March 15, 1973).

CHAPTER I

1. George Tucker, workshop at the Highlander Research and Education Center (1970).
2. Rep. Ken Hechler, speaking to the Senate Committee on Interior and Insular Affairs (March 13, 1973).
3. Thomas N. Bethell, *The Hurricane Creek Massacre* (New York: Harper & Row, 1972).
4. Warren Wright, People's Hearing on Strip Mining, Wise, Virginia (Dec. 4, 1971).
5. John Tiller, tape recording by Helen Lewis for the Commission on Religion in Appalachia.
6. Jean Ritchie, keynote address to the Council of the Southern Mountains, Lake Junaluska (spring, 1970).
7. David Welsh, "Death in Kentucky," in Thomas R. Frazier, ed., *The Underside of American History* (New York: Harcourt Brace Jovanovich, 1973).
8. J. T. Begley, in "Echo of Anger," ABC film (1972).
9. Mike Clark, *Strip Mining in East Kentucky*, Highlander Research and Education Center report (June, 1971).
10. James Branscome, interview (spring, 1973).

11. Wendell Berry, "Mayhem in the Industrial Paradise," *A Continuous Harmony* (New York: Harcourt Brace Jovanovich, 1972).
12. Mike Clark, interview (Nov., 1973).
13. Ralph Hatch, in "Echo of Anger," ABC film.
14. Aubrey J. Wagner, as reported by Ben A. Franklin in *The New York Times* (1965).
15. James Branscome, in "Echo of Anger," ABC film.
16. Donald MacIntosh, observing a reclamation job in Knott County, as reported by David Welsh in "Death in Kentucky," *op. cit.*
17. Joe Begley, in "Echo of Anger," ABC film.
18. Mike Clark, *Strip Mining in East Kentucky*, *op. cit.*
19. Mike Clark, *Strip Mining in East Kentucky*, *op. cit.*
20. Mike Clark, *Strip Mining in East Kentucky*, *op. cit.*
21. Dan Gibson (1st paragraph), as quoted by Bill Peterson, *Coaltown Revisited: An Appalachian Notebook* (Chicago: Henry Regnery, 1972); (2nd paragraph), as quoted by Harry M. Caudill, *My Land Is Dying* (New York: E. P. Dutton, 1973).
22. Joe Mulloy, interview (spring, 1973).
23. Harry M. Caudill, *My Land Is Dying, op. cit.*
24. Thomas N. Bethell, "Hot Time Ahead," in David Walls and John Stephenson, eds., *Appalachia in the Sixties* (Lexington: The University Press of Kentucky, 1972).
25. Eula Hall, workshop at the Highlander Research and Education Center (spring, 1973).
26. Bessie Smith Gayheart, People's Hearing on Strip Mining, Wise, Virginia (Dec. 4, 1971).

CHAPTER II

1. Anna Bland, as quoted by Todd Gitlin and Nanci Hollander in *Uptown: Poor Whites in Chicago* (New York: Harper & Row, 1970).
2. John Arms, interview (spring, 1973).

3. Tom Duff, as quoted by David Holwerk, "Interstate 75: A Morality Play," *Nation* (Nov. 20, 1972).
4. John Arms, *op. cit.*
5. Gurney Norman, *Divine Right's Trip* (New York: Dial Press, 1972).
6. Eula Hall, workshop at the Highlander Research and Education Center (spring, 1973).
7. Hazel Dickens, "As Country As I Could Sing," *Mountain Life and Work* (Dec., 1972).
8. John Arms, *op. cit.*
9. Doug Youngblood, interview (spring, 1973).
10. Doug Youngblood, *op. cit.*
11. Ras Bryant, as quoted by Todd Gitlin and Nanci Hollander in *Uptown: Poor Whites in Chicago, op. cit.*
12. Jim Cornett, in the *Mountain Eagle* (March 15, 1973).
13. Jean Ritchie, keynote address to the Council of the Southern Mountains, Lake Junaluska (spring, 1970).

CHAPTER III

1. Everette Tharp, interview (spring, 1973).
2. Ad in *The New Republic* in the late 1960s, placed by an Office of Economic Opportunity project in Mingo County, West Virginia.
3. Don West, *Romantic Appalachia, or Poverty Pays If You Ain't Poor* (Huntington, West Virginia: Appalachian Movement Press).
4. Everette Tharp, critique of the President's Appalachian Regional Commission proposal (May 28, 1964).
5. Michael Kline, recording "The Poverty War Is Dead," album notes.
6. John Arms, interview (spring, 1973).
7. Buck Maggard, interview (spring, 1973).
8. *Ibid.*
9. John Arms, *op. cit.*
10. *Ibid.*
11. Buck Maggard, *op. cit.*
12. Michael Kline, *op. cit.*
13. Everette Tharp, interview (spring, 1973).
14. Mike Clark, interview (Nov., 1973).
15. Shelva Thompson, interview (spring, 1973).
16. Eula Hall, workshop at the Highlander Research and Education Center (spring, 1973).
17. Shelva Thompson, *op. cit.*
18. Edith Easterling, interview (spring, 1973).

CHAPTER IV

1. Tillman Cadle, interview by Anne Hopkins (1972).
2. George Tucker, workshop at Highlander Research and Education Center (1970).
3. Jake Easterling, interview by Claudia Guyton (fall, 1970).
4. Jim Hamilton, interview by Claudia Guyton (fall, 1970).
5. Jim Jackson, as quoted by Helen Lewis, Clinch Valley College, in her studies of coal miners.
6. Thomas N. Bethell, *The Hurricane Creek Massacre* (New York: Harper & Row, 1972).
7. Nimrod Workman, workshop at the Highlander Research and Education Center (Oct., 1972).
8. Sarah Ogan Gunning, workshop at the Highlander Research and Education Center (Oct., 1972).
9. Nimrod Workman, *op. cit.*
10. Florence Reece, video tape made by Ted Carpenter, Broadside TV.
11. Tillman Cadle, workshop at the Highlander Research and Education Center (Oct., 1972).
12. Jack Hill, *The Labor Defender* (1932; reprinted by Appalachian Movement Press, Huntington, West Virginia).
13. Myles Horton, workshop at the Highlander Research and Education Center (Oct., 1972).

CHAPTER V

1. John L. Lewis, fighting for the UMWA Welfare Fund, 1947, as quoted by A. Britton Hume, *Death and the Mines* (New York: Grossman, 1971).
2. Ben A. Franklin, "The Scandal of Death and Injury in the Mines," in David Walls and John Stephenson, eds., *Appalachia in the Sixties* (Lexington: The University Press of Kentucky, 1972).

3. Jim Hamilton, interview by Claudia Guyton (fall, 1970).
4. *Ibid.*
5. Mrs. Judith Ann Henderson, in *Mountain Life and Work* (Dec., 1970).
6. A. Britton Hume, *Death and the Mines, op. cit.*
7. Thomas N. Bethell, *The Hurricane Creek Massacre* (New York: Harper & Row, 1972).
8. A. T. Collins, video tape made by Ted Carpenter, Broadside TV.
9. Thomas N. Bethell, *Coal Patrol* (Nov. 24, 1971).
10. A. T. Collins, *op. cit.*
11. From *Disaster on Buffalo Creek: A Citizens' Report on Criminal Negligence in a West Virginia Mining Community* (1972).
12. Thomas N. Bethell, *Coal Patrol* (March 1, 1972).
13. Pittston spokesman, *Coal Patrol* (April 24, 1972).
14. U.S. Geological Survey, *Coal Patrol* (April 24, 1972).
15. Thomas N. Bethell, *Coal Patrol* (March 1, 1972).
16. Thomas N. Bethell, *Coal Patrol* (April 24 and May 1, 1972).
17. From *Report to the Shareholders of Pittston* (March 12, 1973).
18. Mike Trbovich, in the *Mountain Eagle* (March 15, 1973).
19. From *Disaster on Buffalo Creek: A Citizens' Report . . .* , *op. cit.*

CHAPTER VI

1. John Tiller, People's Hearing on Strip Mining (Dec. 4, 1971).
2. Buck Maggard, interview (spring, 1973).
3. Everette Tharp, interview (spring, 1973).
4. Clara Sullivan, letter to the *Progressive Labor News* (Jan., 1963).
5. Buck Maggard, *op. cit.*
6. Buck Maggard, *op. cit.*
7. Everette Tharp, *op. cit.*
8. Everette Tharp, "The History, Goals and Objectives of the Appalachian Committee for Full Employment" (1965).
9. Dr. Lorin E. Kerr, speaking at a United Mine Workers convention in 1968.
10. Nimrod Workman, workshop at the Highlander Research and Education Center (Oct., 1972).
11. Bill Worthington, interview (spring, 1973).
12. Donald Rasmussen, interview (spring, 1973).

13. Bill Peterson, *Coaltown Revisited: An Appalachian Notebook* (Chicago: Henry Regnery, 1972).
14. Bill Worthington, *op. cit.*
15. Jim Hamilton, interview by Claudia Guyton (fall, 1970).
16. Jim Hamilton, printed flier.
17. Donald Rasmussen, *op. cit.*
18. Arnold Miller, campaign statement, *Mountain Messenger* (May–June, 1972).
19. Joseph Yablonski, as quoted by Jeanne Rasmussen, "Jock Yablonski's Democracy" (June 15, 1970).
20. Lewis Coleman, *Miner's Voice* (Dec., 1970).
21. Joseph Yablonski, as quoted by Jeanne Rasmussen, "The Spotlight of Truth" (Feb. 4, 1970), and by Bill Peterson, *Coaltown Revisited, op. cit.*
22. Joseph A. "Chip" Yablonski, speaking before the Senate Labor Subcommittee (Feb. 5, 1970).
23. Thomas N. Bethell, *Coal Patrol* (June 1, 1972).
24. Nimrod Workman, workshop at the Highlander Research and Education Center (Oct., 1972).
25. Thomas N. Bethell, *Coal Patrol* (Jan. 1, 1973).
26. *Ibid.*
27. Bill Worthington, *op. cit.*
28. Eddie Burke, *Miner's Voice* (winter, 1973).
29. *UMWA Journal* (Sept., 1973). Additional information from UMWA advertisements and fliers.
30. Darrell Deaton, speaking at the Citizens' Public Inquiry, Evarts, Kentucky, March, 1974.
31. James Turner, speaking at the Inquiry.
32. Lois Scott, speaking at the Inquiry.
33. Harry Patrick, *UMWA Journal* (Sept. 1–15, 1974).
34. Jerry Johnson, *UMWA Journal* (Sept. 1–15, 1974).

BETTER LISTEN TO THE VOICES FROM THE MOUNTAINS

1. Warren Wright, People's Hearing on Strip Mining (Dec. 4, 1971).
2. Rep. Ken Hechler, speaking to Committee on Interior and Insular Affairs (March 13, 1973).
3. Eula Hall, workshop at the Highlander Research and Education Center (spring, 1973).

4. Buck Maggard, interview (spring, 1973).
5. Everette Tharp, interview (spring, 1973).
6. Shelva Thompson, interview (spring, 1973).
7. Arnold Miller, reacting to an accident in West Virginia (Ittman No. 3) (Dec., 1972). Reported by *Coal Patrol* (Jan. 1, 1973).
8. James Branscome, *Mountain Eagle* (Jan. 4, 1973).
9. Tom Gish, speaking at the Fortieth Anniversary Celebration of the Highlander Research and Education Center (Aug., 1972).

A NOTE ABOUT THE EDITORS

Guy and Candie Carawan have spent the last eight years living and working in the Appalachian region. They are the editors of the widely praised book about the people of Johns Island, South Carolina, *Ain't You Got a Right to the Tree of Life*, and two books on the Southern freedom struggle, *We Shall Overcome* (Guy brought the song to the movement) and *Freedom Is a Constant Struggle*.

Guy is the music director of Highlander Center in Tennessee and from 1968 to 1974 was Folklorist-in-Residence at Pitzer College in Claremont, California. He has produced eight documentary LP records on the civil rights movement, Sea Island life, and Appalachian coal miners and has recorded twelve albums of contemporary and traditional folk music. Over the years, he has appeared at many of the major folk festivals, and has traveled here and abroad giving hundreds of concerts. Candie is a potter and artist as well as a singer (she often appears in concert with Guy). The Carawans live in Tennessee with their two children, Evan and Heather.

A NOTE ON THE TYPE

The text of this book was set in Electra, a typeface designed by William Addison Dwiggins for the Mergenthaler Linotype Company and first made available in 1935. Electra cannot be classified as either "modern" or "old-style." It is not based on any historical model, and hence does not echo any particular period or style of type design. It avoids the extreme contrast between thick and thin elements that marks most modern faces, and is without eccentricities which catch the eye and interfere with reading. In general, Electra is a simple, readable type face that attempts to give a feeling of fluidity, power, and speed.

W. A. Dwiggins (1880–1956) began an association with the Mergenthaler Linotype Company in 1929 and over the next twenty-seven years designed a number of book types, the most interesting of which are the Metro series, Electra, Caledonia, Eldorado, and Falcon.

Composed by Kingsport Press, Inc., Kingsport, Tenn.
Printed by Halliday Lithograph Corp., West Hanover, Mass., and bound by American Book–Stratford Press, Saddle Brook, N.J.

Calligraphy by David Lindroth
Music drawn by Volker Zinser
Typography and binding design by Virginia Tan